Ordnance Survey
Norfo~~l~~
Suffolk ~~Walks~~

Pathfinder Guide

Compiled by John Brooks   Series editor: Brian Conduit

Key to colour coding

The walks are divided into three broad categories. These differ slightly from the categories in other Pathfinder guides, to take account of the terrain in Norfolk and Suffolk. They are indicated by the following colours:

Short, easy walks

Walks of moderate length, often over more difficult terrain

Longer, more challenging walks

Acknowledgements

I would like to thank Peter Dugdale of Norfolk County Council and Brian Newton of Suffolk County Council for their help and advice in checking the definitive maps. Richard Partington, Mary Muir and Declan Keiley of the Broads Authority also gave valuable assistance, as did Keith Zealand (National Trust), Marcus Galey (South Norfolk District Council), and Peter Morrow (Bungay Town Council).

Ordnance Survey ISBN 0-319-00245-4
Jarrold Publishing ISBN 0-7117-0551-8

First published 1991 by Ordnance Survey and Jarrold Publishing
Reprinted 1993

Ordnance Survey   Jarrold Publishing
Romsey Road   Whitefriars
Maybush   Norwich NR3 1TR
Southampton SO9 4DH

© Crown copyright 1991

Printed in Great Britain by Jarrold Printing, Norwich. 2/93

Previous page: *Blickling Hall, an outstanding example of Jacobean architecture*

Contents

Introduction to Norfolk and Suffolk		4
The National Parks and countryside recreation		6
The Broads National Park		8
The National Trust		9
The Ramblers' Association		9
Walkers and the law		10
Countryside Access Charter		11
Key maps		12
Conventional signs		16

Walks

1	Clare	18
2	Orford Castle and river	19
3	Castle Rising and the Wootton commons	21
4	Dunwich Heath and Minsmere	22
5	Constable Country	24
6	Bungay, Bath Hills and the Bigod Way	26
7	Lavenham and Brent Eleigh	28
8	Walberswick marshes and common	29
9	Castle Acre and the River Nar valley	31
10	The Weavers Way and Dilham Canal	32
11	The Raynhams	34
12	Hoxne — St Edmund's village	36
13	River Waveney walk	38
14	The Tattingstone Wonder and Stutton Ness	40
15	Blickling Park and the upper Bure valley	42
16	Houghton, Harpley and the Peddars Way	45
17	Five south Norfolk villages	48
18	River Bure walk	50
19	Pingoland and Thompson Water	52
20	Knettishall Heath and Thetford Forest	54
21	An Orwell walk from Pin Mill	56
22	'Ted Ellis Country'	58
23	Nelson's boyhood home and Holkham Park	61
24	Berney Arms and Breydon Water	64
25	Framlingham and Earl Soham	66
26	Marriott's Way and Drayton Drewray	69
27	Sheringham Park and Pretty Corner	72
28	Thorpeness, Friston and the Sailors' Path	75

Useful organisations		78
Ordnance Survey maps of Norfolk and Suffolk		78
Index		79

Introduction to Norfolk and Suffolk

Many walkers, tired of the overcrowded routes of the best-known walking counties, are seeking challenges in countryside new to them. Those used to the hill paths and rock scrambles of Derbyshire or the Lakes may turn up their noses at the prospect of exploring the seemingly flat and featureless counties of Norfolk and Suffolk. This would be unfortunate, however, for although there are no taxing gradients or spectacular high viewpoints there is much to be discovered here.

The landscape cannot boast the natural features which give our highland regions their appeal. Instead it is man who has adapted it for his purposes, and without the effect of his activities over the countless generations since prehistoric times there would be little of interest other than an interminable and impenetrable forest.

This hyperactive woodland was generated by an exceptionally rich soil. It probably took the earliest farmers some time to discover this, since access into the forest was difficult. The easiest way was to use the rivers which strike deep into the heartland of the two counties, but there was also the remarkable prehistoric thoroughfare which followed a series of chalk ridges from Wiltshire to the coast of the Wash near Hunstanton. It gave our ancestors access to the fertile ground at the foot of the chalk ridge and to Grimes Graves, the prehistoric flint mines which were East Anglia's earliest industry. Flint, which was at first worked solely for use as cutting edges and arrow-heads, later became valuable as the only building stone to be found in the region with the exception of the soft carrstone of north-west Norfolk.

The Romans came to Norfolk and Suffolk, saw the two counties, and left them largely untouched, apart from placing garrisons at strategic points and establishing a network of roads. The most important of these was the Peddars Way which runs parallel to the Icknield Way to reach the coast at Holme next the Sea. East Anglia played a significant role in events through the Dark Ages. The Vikings were frequent visitors to the region and their influence lingers in the place-names as well as in the fair hair and complexions of their descendants.

The Normans were more powerful and influential invaders and left more obvious monuments. Their great castles and cathedrals remain as testimony to their power, though smaller castles, little more than stockades raised on earthen hillocks

(mottes), can be seen better on the map than on the ground and are plentifully spread about the two counties. The Normans founded many abbeys as well as churches and their contribution to our cultural heritage is magnificently apparent all over East Anglia. It was probably about this time that men began to cut peat from the great fens of south-east Norfolk, a process which continued until Tudor times when it became impossible to cut any more peat for fuel. Water filled the diggings and so created a series of large, shallow, inland lakes – the Norfolk and Suffolk Broads.

The keep of Orford Castle dates from 1165

Throughout these centuries landowners and their serfs had been assiduously clearing back the woodland and turning the land over to arable farming. The end of the thirteenth century was the time of the region's greatest prosperity. Sheep farming and the textile industry flourished and both weavers and the owners of the sheep prospered. They built large houses for themselves in towns and villages, and gave thanks to God for their fortune by building a host of churches of matchless splendour. Although the Black Death brought a sudden and dreadful pause to the growing prosperity in the mid-fourteenth century – there are several villages in Norfolk and Suffolk which were abandoned at this time – the wool trade continued to flourish and brought the two counties the most enduring part of their heritage.

Apart from churches and a handful of important secular buildings most buildings of this time were constructed of timber and clay. Where the wealthy merchants built their new houses with a stout timber framework, infilling with clay lump, the peasants lived in cottages of wattle and daub. This method of construction, still used in these parts within living memory, meant that puddled clay was daubed around a brushwood framework. Many cottages in Norfolk and Suffolk built in this way are still standing after more than 200 years, albeit now usually reinforced by breeze blocks.

Bricks began to be used in the building of grand houses in early Tudor times when many of the wealthier merchants acquired large estates. The majority of the stately homes of Norfolk and Suffolk, built in later centuries, are of brick, which has been weathered over the years into a mellowness that blends perfectly with the landscape.

The end of the Tudor era saw the region still prosperous, though Norwich was declining in importance — at one time in the Middle Ages it was second largest city in the land. This was due to the fall in fortune of the wool trade — finer cloths could be imported. Cromwell's men had a field-day during the Civil War, running riot through the richly decorated churches and smashing any object of art that struck them as being idolatrous. The decline continued through the next century when Enclosure Acts meant that the old commons, which in theory belonged to a parish, were fenced off arbitrarily by wealthy landowners, thus forcing people from the land. When, in the nineteenth century, agriculture suffered severe economic decline, yet more people were turned off the land. Many were drawn to the growing industries of the big cities, while some followed the pattern set by Scotland and Ireland and emigrated. Thousands of cottages and smallholdings were left to decay.

The arrival of the railways in the eastern counties brought a new importance to many rural communities. Out-of-the-way backwaters like Melton Constable in north Norfolk suddenly became places of significance in railway timetables. By the end of the nineteenth century railways had brought a different way of life to most villages: newspapers could be delivered every day and country people were able to reach the nearest market town much more easily.

In the same way the latter part of the twentieth century has seen another change which has been just as significant. The mobility given by the motor car has made a host of villages dormitories for such places as Norwich and Ipswich, while fast trains mean that many people live in Norfolk and Suffolk and commute to London. There are even said to be people who live in Norfolk and work in Amsterdam. Those who commute to London from Norfolk and Suffolk prove an essential truth: though it may be expensive and uncomfortable to have to undertake such journeys, it is worthwhile just to live in such attractive surroundings.

These changes in our patterns of living have wrought parallel changes in the

The lonely Halvergate Marshes

landscape. Although there are no motorways in Norfolk or Suffolk there are plenty of broad new trunk roads and bypasses. In most cases these improve life by relieving pretty villages of the burdens of traffic, though occasionally this is at the expense of the surrounding countryside. Other changes are more subtle. Modern agricultural practice has meant a demand for larger and larger fields and thus countless hedgerows have vanished as farmers strive for more viable acreages. Sometimes a few trees remain as a monument to a lost hedgerow but usually no trace exists unless a right of way followed the field edge. In that case the path now strikes straight across a vast field: if it has a crop this often presents the walker with a considerable problem.

The responsibility for keeping footpaths in existence rests on the shoulders of the public, and if the paths are used they will survive. An intrepid walker's footprints on a right of way across a vast newly planted field will encourage others to follow, and though it is up to farmers to reinstate footpaths and keep them cleared it is unrealistic to expect them to do so if they believe that the paths are never used. Following the correct lines of the routes in these circumstances is important and will need careful map-reading. Avoid detours unless it is completely unavoidable; most of the routes in this book are on well established paths and there are only a few instances where there are long fields to cross. Serious problems should be reported to the highways department of the county council concerned, whose duty it is to remedy matters.

Despite the changes brought about by agriculture and the elements — Suffolk's trees suffered particularly badly from the hurricane in 1987 as well as in subsequent storms — parts of the two counties remain almost as lovely as when they were painted by Constable, Cotman or Crome. These artists recognised the importance of the sky in East Anglian scenery and magnificent skies can often glorify a somewhat flat and featureless landscape.

Nowhere is this feeling stronger than on the coast, where the clarity of the North Sea light is another element which delights artists. 'On a clear day − and they are mostly clear days in this part of the world − you can see as far as you can bear to see, and sometimes further', wrote Ronald Blythe in *Akenfield*.

Another East Anglian characteristic runs hand in hand with this sparkling light. This is the keenness of the easterly winds. As locals will have it, there are no sheltering mountains between here and central Russia. Be warned, then, that it may seem quite warm on emerging from the car, but on the shore, or on the flood bank of Breydon Water, it may well feel bitterly cold.

Beware too of exposing knees. Brambles and nettles in Norfolk and Suffolk snatch at every inch of exposed flesh. Footpaths can quickly become choked by their growth so shorts are not advisable. Although in a dry summer it will be possible to walk many of these routes in trainers, hiking boots are the best bet overall. Wellingtons are all right up to about five miles but after that will prove hot and chafing. Many of the paths and tracks serve also as bridleways and can become very boggy if the local hunt or riding school has passed recently.

Both counties have long coastlines, these being extended by the network of rivers and inland lakes which comprise the Broads of Norfolk and Suffolk, and in the latter by the long estuaries of the rivers Blyth, Alde, Deben, Orwell and Stour. Coast paths run alongside much of this shoreline, providing excellent walking as well as opportunities for birdwatching.

Other long-distance paths mainly belong to Norfolk. The Peddars Way traverses the county from south to north, going across the sandy heaths of Breckland to reach the 'uplands' of west Norfolk − one of the least-frequented parts of the county. From here it continues northwards to the coast at Holme next the Sea near Hunstanton and then links with the Norfolk Coast Path, striking eastwards to Cromer, a total distance of 93 miles (149 km). The Weavers Way, another long-distance path, starts at Cromer and ends at Great Yarmouth, a further 56 miles (90 km). From Yarmouth the long-distance walker can continue along the Angles Way, which skirts Breydon Water to follow the delightful Waveney valley westwards, joining with the Peddars Way again at Knettishall Heath, a circuit of 220 miles (352 km) which makes up the marathon Around Norfolk Walk. Suffolk also promotes a footpath following the course of the Waveney − the Waveney Way − which is 70 miles (112 km)

Typical Norfolk cottage at Ashwellthorpe

long and includes some of the Angles Way route. Parts of most of these long-distance paths are used in walks in this book.

Suffolk is the starting point for one of the most famous and ancient of Britain's thoroughfares − the Icknield Way. Starting in the north of the county near Brandon it traverses 104 miles (166 km) of southern England, nearly a third of it in Suffolk.

All that remains is to wish the reader good walking. May the weather be kind and the going easy. There is infinite enjoyment to be had from this countryside where, to quote Ronald Blythe again, 'the scenery carries undulation to the most subtle limits'.

The National Parks and countryside recreation

Ten National Parks were created in England and Wales as a result of an Act of Parliament in 1949, and an eleventh was established under special legislation in 1989. In addition to these, there are numerous specially designated Areas of Outstanding Natural Beauty, Country and Regional Parks, Sites of Special Scientific Interest and picnic areas scattered throughout England, Wales and Scotland, all of which share the twin aims of preservation of the countryside and public accessibility and enjoyment.

In trying to define a National Park, one point to bear in mind is that unlike many overseas ones, Britain's National Parks are not owned by the nation. The vast bulk of the land in them is under private ownership. John Dower, whose report in 1945 created their framework, defined a National Park as 'an extensive area of beautiful and relatively wild country in which, for the nation's benefit and by appropriate national decision and action, (a) the characteristic landscape beauty is strictly preserved, (b) access and facilities for public open-air enjoyment are amply provided, (c) wildlife and buildings and places of architectural and historic interest are suitably protected, while (d) established farming use is effectively maintained'.

The concept of having designated areas of protected countryside grew out of a number of factors that appeared towards the end of the nineteenth century; principally greater facilities and opportunities for travel, the development of various conservationist bodies and the establishment of National Parks abroad. Apart from a few of the early individual travellers such as Celia Fiennes and Daniel Defoe, who were usually more concerned with commenting on agricultural improvements, the appearance of towns and the extent of antiquities to be found than with the wonders of nature, interest in the countryside as a source of beauty, spiritual refreshment and recreation, and, along with that, an interest in conserving it, did not arise until the Victorian era. Towards the end of the eighteenth century, improvements in road transport enabled the wealthy to visit regions that had hitherto been largely inaccessible and, by the middle of the nineteenth century, the construction of the railways opened up such possibilities to the middle classes and, later on, to the working classes in even greater numbers. At the same time, the Romantic movement was in full swing and, encouraged by the works of Wordsworth, Coleridge and Shelley, interest and enthusiasm for wild places, including the mountain, moorland and hill regions of northern and western Britain, were now in vogue. Eighteenth-century taste had thought of the Scottish Highlands, the Lake District and Snowdonia as places to avoid, preferring controlled order and symmetry in nature as well as in architecture and town planning. But upper and middle class Victorian travellers were thrilled and awed by what they saw as the untamed savagery and wilderness of mountain peaks, deep and secluded gorges, thundering waterfalls, towering cliffs and rocky crags. In addition, there was a growing reaction against the materialism and squalor of Victorian industrialisation and urbanisation and a desire to escape from the formality and artificiality of town life into areas of unspoilt natural beauty.

A result of this was the formation of a number of different societies, all concerned with the 'great outdoors': naturalist groups, rambling clubs and conservationist organisations. One of the earliest of these was the Commons, Open Spaces and Footpaths Preservation Society, originally founded in 1865 to preserve commons and develop public access to the countryside. Particularly influential was the National Trust, set up in 1895 to protect and maintain both places of natural beauty and places of historic interest, and, later on, the Councils for the Preservation of Rural England, Wales and Scotland, three separate bodies that came into being between 1926 and 1928.

The world's first National Park was the Yellowstone Park in the United States, designated in 1872. This was followed by others in Canada, South Africa, Germany, Switzerland, New Zealand and elsewhere, but in Britain such places did not come about until after the Second World War. Proposals for the creation of areas of protected countryside were made before the First World War and during the 1920s and 1930s, but nothing was done. The growing demand from people in towns for access to open country and the reluctance of landowners — particularly those who owned large expanses of uncultivated moorland — to grant it led to a number of ugly incidents, in particular the mass trespass in the Peak District in 1932, when fighting took place between ramblers and gamekeepers and some of the trespassers received stiff prison sentences.

It was in the climate exemplified by the Beveridge Report and the subsequent creation of the welfare state, however, that calls for countryside conservation and access came to fruition in parliament. Based on the recommendations of the Dower Report (1945) and the Hobhouse Committee (1947), the National Parks and Countryside Act of 1949 provided for the designation and preservation of areas both of great scenic beauty and of particular wildlife and scientific interest throughout Britain. More specifically it provided for the creation of National Parks in England and Wales. Scotland was excluded because, with greater areas of open space and a smaller population, there were fewer pressures on the Scottish countryside and therefore there was felt to be less need for the creation of such protected areas.

A National Parks Commission was set up, and over the next eight years ten areas were designated as parks; seven in England (Northumberland, Lake District, North York Moors, Yorkshire Dales, Peak District, Exmoor and Dartmoor) and three in Wales (Snowdonia, Brecon Beacons and Pembrokeshire Coast). At the same time the Commission was also given the responsibility for designating other smaller areas of high recreational and scenic qualities (Areas of Outstanding Natural Beauty), plus the power to propose and develop long-distance footpaths, now called National Trails, though it was not until 1965 that the first of these, the Pennine Way, came into existence.

Further changes came with the Countryside Act of 1968 (a similar one for Scotland had been passed in 1967). The National Parks Commission was replaced by the Countryside Commission, which was now to oversee and review virtually all aspects of countryside conservation, access and provision of recreational amenities. The Country Parks, which were smaller areas of countryside often close to urban areas, came into being. A number of long-distance footpaths were created, followed by an even greater number of unofficial long- or middle-distance paths, devised by individuals, ramblers' groups or local authorities. Provision of car parks and visitor centres, waymarking of public rights of way and the production of leaflets giving suggestions for walking routes all increased, a reflection both of increased leisure and of a greater desire for recreational activity, of which walking in particular, now recognised as the most popular leisure pursuit, has had a great explosion of interest.

In 1989 the Norfolk and Suffolk Broads joined the National Park family, special legislation being passed to cover the area's navigational interests as well as aspects of conservation and public enjoyment.

The authorities who administer the individual National Parks have the very difficult task of reconciling the interests of the people who live and earn their living within them with those of the visitors. National Parks, and the other designated areas, are not living museums. Developments of various kinds, in housing, transport and rural industries, are needed. There is pressure to exploit the resources of the area, through more intensive farming, or through increased quarrying and forestry, extraction of minerals or the construction of reservoirs.

In the end it all comes down to a question of balance; a balance between conservation and 'sensitive development'. On the one hand there is a responsibility to preserve and enhance the natural beauty of the National Parks and to promote their enjoyment by the public, and on the other, the needs and well-being of the people living and working in them have to be borne in mind.

The Broads National Park

The Broads is Britain's newest and very special National Park. Established by the Broads Act in April 1989, it is Britain's only lowland, wetland National Park. It is also the country's largest, most famous inland waterway, containing 125 miles (200 km) of navigable rivers and lakes, or broads. Like the ten other National Parks in Britain, the Broads is protected because of its rich wildlife, unique landscape, and the recreational opportunities it offers.

Wide, dramatic skies, slow, winding rivers, broads, reedbeds, tangled woodlands and windswept grazing marshes are just some of the features which make the Broads' landscape so special. The old windpumps and traditional buildings also contribute to its unique character. The Broads is a haven for wildlife, supporting many species of plants, insects and birds – the swallowtail butterfly and the Norfolk Aeshna dragonfly are found nowhere else in Britain. There are superb opportunities for recreation and leisure, including boating, birdwatching, walking and cycling.

The Broads is managed by the Broads Authority, a statutory organisation reconstituted in April 1989. Unlike many National Parks abroad, National Parks in Britain are places where people live and work, and this inevitably places conflicting demands upon the environment. The Broads Authority is responsible for ensuring that the needs of conserving the Broads, protecting local people's interests, protecting the rights of navigation and ensuring that visitors can enjoy the Broads are all carefully and sensitively balanced.

As part of the European Natural Sites Twinning Programme, the Broads is twinned with two similar wetland areas in Europe, the Audomarois Regional Park in France and the Weerribben National Park in the Netherlands. Over a million people visit the Broads each year. The Broads Authority operates three Broads tourist information centres, and each year organises an events programme, called Fun in the Broads, which includes boat trips, guided walks, cycle rides, archive films and

The River Bure and Oby Mill

puppet shows, with the aim of offering people of all ages the opportunity to discover and enjoy the wildlife, landscape and beauty of the Broads. The programme runs from April to October.

Walking is an ideal way to explore the Broads and there are many lovely walks to choose from. They vary in length from short strolls to, for example, the long-distance Weavers Way footpath. The Broads Authority establishes and waymarks walks in the Broads, and a series of waymarked walks and accompanying leaflets are available for the Bure, Ant and Thurne valleys. Waymarked walks are also being established in the Yare and Waveney valleys.

Broads Authority Information Centres are open from Easter to September/October. Their addresses are on page 78.

The National Trust

Anyone who likes visiting places of natural beauty and/or historic interest has cause to be grateful to the National Trust. Without it, many such places would probably have vanished by now, either under an avalanche of concrete and bricks and mortar or through reservoir construction or blanket afforestation.

It was in response to the pressures on the countryside posed by the relentless march of Victorian industrialisation that the Trust was set up in 1895. Its founders, inspired by the common goals of protecting and conserving Britain's national heritage and widening public access to it, were Sir Robert Hunter, Octavia Hill and Canon Rawnsley; a solicitor, a social reformer and a clergyman respectively. The latter was particularly influential. As a canon of Carlisle Cathedral and vicar of Crosthwaite (near Keswick), he was concerned about threats to the Lake District and had already been active in protecting footpaths and promoting public access to open countryside. After the flooding of Thirlmere in 1879 to create a large reservoir, he and his two colleagues became increasingly convinced that the only effective protection was outright ownership of land.

The purpose of the National Trust is to preserve areas of natural beauty and sites of historic interest by acquisition, holding them in trust for the nation and making them available for public access and enjoyment. Some of its properties have been acquired through purchase, but many have been donated. Nowadays it is not only one of the biggest landowners in the country, but also one of the most active conservation charities,

The Little Ouse River at Knettishall

protecting well over half a million acres of land, including over 500 miles of coastline and a large number of historic properties (houses, castles and gardens) in England, Wales and Northern Ireland. (There is a separate National Trust for Scotland, which was set up in 1931.)

Furthermore, once a piece of land has come under Trust ownership, it is difficult for its status to be altered. As a result of Parliamentary legislation in 1907, the Trust was given the right to declare its property inalienable, so ensuring that in any dispute it can appeal directly to Parliament.

As it works towards its dual aims of conserving areas of attractive countryside and encouraging greater public access (not easy to reconcile in this age of mass tourism), the Trust provides an excellent service to walkers by creating new concessionary paths and waymarked trails, by maintaining stiles and footbridges and by combating the ever-increasing problem of footpath erosion.

For details of membership, contact the National Trust at the address on page 78.

The Ramblers' Association

No organisation works more actively to protect and extend the rights and interests of walkers in the countryside than the Ramblers' Association. Its aims (summarised here) are clear: to foster a greater knowledge, love and care of the countryside; to assist in the protection and enhancement of public rights of way and areas of natural beauty; to work for greater public access to the countryside and to encourage more people to take up rambling as a healthy, recreational activity.

It was founded in 1935 when, following the setting up of a National Council of Ramblers'

Federation in 1931, a number of federations earlier formed in London, Manchester, the Midlands and elsewhere came together to create a more effective pressure group, to deal with such contemporary problems as the disappearance and obstruction of footpaths, the prevention of access to open mountain and moorland and increasing hostility from landowners. This was the era of the mass trespasses, when there were sometimes violent confrontations between ramblers and gamekeepers, especially on the moorlands of the Peak District.

Since then the Ramblers' Association has played an influential role in preserving and developing the national footpath network, supporting the creation of National Parks and encouraging the designation and way-marking of long-distance footpaths.

Our freedom to walk in the countryside is precarious, and requires constant vigilance. As well as the perennial problems of footpaths being illegally obstructed, disappearing through lack of use or extinguished by housing or road construction, new dangers can spring up at any time.

It is to meet such problems and dangers that the Ramblers' Association exists and represents the interests of all walkers. The address to write to for information on the Ramblers' Association and how to become a member is given on page 78.

Walkers and the law

The average walker in a National Park or other popular walking area, armed with the appropriate Ordnance Survey map, reinforced perhaps by a guidebook giving detailed walking instructions, is unlikely to run into legal difficulties, but it is useful to know something about the law relating to public rights of way. The right to walk over certain parts of the countryside has developed over a long period of time, and how such rights came into being and how far they are protected by the law is a complex subject, fascinating in its own right, but too lengthy to be discussed here. The following comments are intended simply to be a helpful guide, backed up by the Countryside Access Charter, a concise summary of walkers' rights and obligations drawn up by the Countryside Commission.

Basically there are two main kinds of public rights of way: footpaths (for walkers only) and bridleways (for walkers, riders on horseback and pedal cyclists). Footpaths and bridleways are shown by broken green lines on Ordnance Survey Pathfinder and Outdoor Leisure maps and broken red lines on Landranger maps. There is also a third category, called byways or 'roads used as a public path': chiefly broad, walled tracks (green lanes) or farm roads, which walkers, riders and cyclists have to share, usually only occasionally, with motor vehicles. Many of these public paths have been in existence for hundreds of years and some even originated as prehistoric trackways and have been in constant use for well over 2,000 years.

The term 'right of way' means exactly what it says. It gives right of passage over what, in the vast majority of cases, is private land, and you are required to keep to the line of the path and not stray onto the land either side. If you inadvertently wander off the right of way — either because of faulty map-reading or because the route is not clearly indicated on the ground — you are technically trespassing and the wisest course is to ask the nearest available person (farmer or fellow walker) to direct you back to the correct route. There are stories of unpleasant confrontations between walkers and farmers at times, but in general most farmers are helpful and co-operative when responding to a genuine and polite request for assistance in route finding.

Obstructions can sometimes be a problem and probably the commonest of these is where a path across a field has been ploughed up. It is legal for a farmer to plough up a path provided that he restores it within two weeks, barring exceptionally bad weather. This does not always happen and here the walker is presented with a dilemma. Does he follow the line of the path, even if this inevitably means treading on crops, or does he use his common sense and walk around the edge of the field? The latter course of action often seems the best but, as this means that you would be trespassing, you are, in law, supposed to keep to the exact line of the path, avoiding unnecessary damage to crops. In the case of other obstructions which may block a path (illegal fences and locked gates etc.), common sense again has to be used in order to negotiate them by the easiest method (detour or removal). If you have any problems negotiating rights of way, you should report the matter to the Rights of Way Department of the relevant county, borough or metropolitan district council. They will then take action with the landowner concerned.

Apart from rights of way enshrined by law, there are a number of other paths available to walkers. Permissive or concessionary paths have been created where a landowner has given permission for the public to use a particular route across his land. The main problem with these is that, as they have been granted as a concession, there is no legal right to use them and therefore they can be extinguished at any time. In practice, many of these concessionary routes have been established on land owned either by large public bodies such as the Forestry Commission, or by a private one, such as the National Trust, and as these mainly encourage walkers to use their paths, they are unlikely to be closed unless a change of ownership occurs.

Walkers also have free access to Country Parks (except where requested to keep away from certain areas for ecological reasons, e.g. wildlife protection, woodland regeneration, safeguarding of rare plants etc.), canal towpaths and most beaches. By custom, though not by right, you are generally free to walk across the open and uncultivated higher land of mountain, moorland and fell, but this varies from area to area and from one season to another − grouse moors, for example, will be out of bounds during the breeding and shooting seasons and some open areas are used as Ministry of Defence firing ranges, for which reason access will be restricted. In some areas the situation has been clarified as a result of 'access agreements' between the landowners and either the county council or the National Park authority, which clearly define when and where you can walk over such open country.

Countryside Access Charter

Your rights of way are:
- Public footpaths − on foot only. Sometimes waymarked in yellow
- Bridleways − on foot, horseback and pedal cycle. Sometimes waymarked in blue
- Byways (usually old roads), most 'roads used as public paths' and, of course, public roads − all traffic has the right of way

Use maps, signs and waymarks to check rights of way. Ordnance Survey Pathfinder and Landranger maps show most public rights of way

On rights of way you can:
- take a pram, pushchair or wheelchair if practicable
- take a dog (on a lead or under close control)
- take a short route round an illegal obstruction or remove it sufficiently to get past

Saxtead Mill

You have a right to go for recreation to:
- public parks and open spaces − on foot
- most commons near older towns and cities − on foot and sometimes on horseback
- private land where the owner has a formal agreement with the local authority

In addition you can use the following by local or established custom or consent, but ask for advice if you are unsure:
- many areas of open country, such as moorland, fell and coastal areas, especially those in the care of the National Trust, and some commons
- some woods and forests, especially those owned by the Forestry Commission
- Country Parks and picnic sites
- most beaches
- canal towpaths
- some private paths and tracks

Consent sometimes extends to horse-riding and cycling

For your information:
- county councils and London boroughs maintain and record rights of way, and register commons
- obstructions, dangerous animals, harassment and misleading signs on rights of way are illegal and you should report them to the county council
- paths across fields can be ploughed, but must normally be reinstated within two weeks
- landowners can require you to leave land to which you have no right of access
- motor vehicles are normally permitted only on roads, byways and some 'roads used as public paths'

Key Map 1

Key Map 2

CONVENTIONAL SIGNS
1:25 000 or 2½ INCHES to 1 MILE

ROADS AND PATHS

Not necessarily rights of way

M I or A 6(M)	M I or A 6(M)	Motorway
A 31 (T)	A 31 (T)	Trunk road
A 35	A 35	Main road
B 3074	B 3074	Secondary road
A 35	A 35	Dual carriageway

Narrow roads with passing places are annotated

Road generally more than 4m wide

Road generally less than 4m wide

Other road, drive or track

Unfenced roads and tracks are shown by pecked lines

Path

RAILWAYS

Multiple track	Standard gauge
Single track	
Narrow gauge	
Siding	
Cutting	
Embankment	
Tunnel	
Road over & under	
Level crossing; station	

PUBLIC RIGHTS OF WAY
Public rights of way may not be evident on the ground

Public paths { Footpath / Bridleway

+ + + + + Byway open to all traffic
+ + + + Road used as a public path

DANGER AREA
Firing and test ranges in the area
Danger!
Observe warning notices

The indication of a towpath in this book does not necessarily imply a public right of way
The representation of any other road, track or path is no evidence of the existence of a right of way

BOUNDARIES

— · — · — · — County (England and Wales)

— — — — — District

–o– –o– –o– –o– –o– London Borough

· · · · · · · · · · · · · · Civil Parish (England)* Community (Wales)

– – – – – – – – Constituency (County, Borough, Burgh or European Assembly)

Coincident boundaries are shown by the first appropriate symbol

*For Ordnance Survey purposes County Boundary is deemed to be the limit of the parish structure whether or not a parish area adjoins

SYMBOLS

Place of worship	with tower
	with spire, minaret or dome
+	without such additions

▢ △ Glasshouse; youth hostel

Bus or coach station

Lighthouse; lightship; beacon

Triangulation station

Triangulation point on { church or chapel / lighthouse, beacon / building; chimney

Electricity transmission line
pylon   pole

VILLA — Roman antiquity (AD 43 to AD 420)

Castle — Other antiquities

Site of antiquity

1066 — Site of battle (with date)

Gravel pit

Sand pit

Chalk pit, clay pit or quarry

Refuse or slag heap

Sloping wall

Water | Mud

Sand; sand & shingle

National Park or Forest Park Boundary

NT — National Trust open access

NT — National Trust limited access

NTS NTS — National Trust for Scotland

VEGETATION
Limits of vegetation are defined by positioning of the symbols but may be delineated also by pecks or dots

Coniferous trees

Non-coniferous trees

Coppice

Orchard

Scrub

Marsh, reeds, saltings

Bracken, rough grassland
In some areas bracken (o) and rough grassland (· · · ·) are shown separately

Heath

Shown collectively as rough grassland on some sheets

In some areas reeds ( ) and saltings ( ) are shown separate

HEIGHTS AND ROCK FEATURES

50 } Determined { ground survey
285 } by { air survey

Surface heights are to the nearest metre above mean sea level. Heights shown close to a triangulation pillar refer to the ground level height at the pillar and not necessarily the summit.

Vertical face

Loose rock   Boulders   Outcrop   Scree

Contours are at 5 metres vertical interval

TOURIST INFORMATION

Abbey, Cathedral, Priory	Garden	Other tourist feature
Aquarium	Golf course or links	Picnic site
Camp site	Historic house	Preserved railway
Caravan site	Information centre	Racecourse
Castle	Motor racing	Skiing
Cave	Museum	Viewpoint
Country park	Nature or forest trail	Wildlife park
Craft centre	Nature reserve	Zoo

Parking

PC Public Convenience (in rural areas)

Ancient Monuments and Historic Buildings in the care of the Secretary of State for the Environment which are open to the public.

National trail or Recreational Path
Long Distance Route (Scotland only)

Pennine Way — Named path

Castle / SAILING — Selected places of interest

T — Public telephone

Mountain rescue post

NATIONAL PARK ACCESS LAND — Boundary of National Park access land
Private land for which the National Park Planning Board have negotiated public access

Access Point

WALKS

1 — Start point of walk

Featured walk

Route of walk

Alternative route

ABBREVIATIONS 1:25 000 or $2\frac{1}{2}$ INCHES to 1 MILE also 1:10 000/1:10 560 or 6 INCHES to 1 MILE

BP,BS	Boundary Post or Stone	P	Post Office	A,R	Telephone, AA or RAC
CH	Club House	Pol Sta	Police Station	TH	Town Hall
F V	Ferry Foot or Vehicle	PC	Public Convenience	Twr	Tower
FB	Foot Bridge	PH	Public House	W	Well
HO	House	Sch	School	Wd Pp	Wind Pump
MP,MS	Mile Post or Stone	Spr	Spring		
Mon	Monument	T	Telephone, public		

Abbreviations applicable only to 1:10 000/1:10 560 or 6 INCHES to 1 MILE

Ch	Church	GP	Guide Post	TCB	Telephone Call Box
F Sta	Fire Station	P	Pole or Post	TCP	Telephone Call Post
Fn	Fountain	S	Stone	Y	Youth Hostel

FOLLOW THE COUNTRY CODE

Enjoy the countryside and respect its life and work

Guard against all risk of fire

Fasten all gates

Keep your dogs under close control

Keep to public paths across farmland

Leave livestock, crops and machinery alone

Use gates and stiles to cross fences, hedges and walls

Take your litter home

Help to keep all water clean

Protect wildlife, plants and trees

Take special care on country roads

Make no unnecessary noise

Reproduced by permission of the Countryside Commission

1 Clare

Start:	Clare
Distance:	3½ miles (5·5 km)
Approximate time:	2 hours
Parking:	Clare Castle Country Park car park
Refreshments:	Pubs and tearooms at Clare
Ordnance Survey maps:	Landranger 155 (Bury St Edmunds & Sudbury) and Pathfinder 1028, TL 64/74 (Haverhill & Clare)

General description *A surprising amount of history is packed into the small town of Clare in south Suffolk. It is dominated by the remains of its castle, the shattered walls of the thirteenth-century keep standing atop the magnificent Norman motte. The bailey walls surrounded 20 acres: steps and paths from the Country Park lead up to the barbican and shell of the keep − a fine viewpoint. To the north is Clare Camp, an earlier fortification probably dating from the second century AD. The walk circles Clare and allows views of the ancient buildings of the town from the surrounding countryside. Note that dogs are not allowed into the Country Park (a detour is suggested for walkers with dogs).*

Turn to the west from the car park (right as you face the river) and cross the old railway bridge which took the line from Haverhill to Long Melford over the River Stour. The route now follows the railway track alongside the river, allowing views of the backs of some of Clare's fine old houses. When the track meets the road turn right, following the circular walk logo, to cross the bridge.

Continue to the top of the road and cross the main Haverhill to Long Melford road by turning left and then immediately right onto a track. This becomes a path, turning right towards the church and passing behind old houses. It crosses the entrance of a graveyard to a kissing-gate. The field-edge path bears left away from an enclosed path and soon joins with a good track heading into open country.

There are exceptional views all round though few hedges are to be seen. The track climbs gradually, passing a dead tree − a

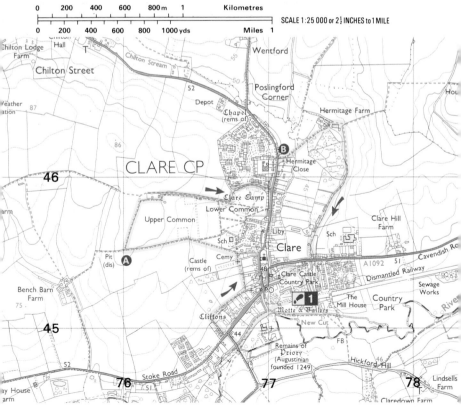

Clare from the castle mound

2 Orford Castle and river

Start:	Orford
Distance:	4 miles (6·5 km)
Approximate time:	2 hours
Parking:	Orford — car park off B1084 just before quay
Refreshments:	Pubs, restaurants and tearooms at Orford
Ordnance Survey maps:	Landranger 156 (Saxmundham & Aldeburgh) and 169 (Ipswich & The Naze) and Pathfinder 1009, TM 44/45 (Aldeburgh & Orford)

General description *This is a short route which combines the opportunity of exploring the many historical features of Orford with a bracing walk along the riverbank to Chantry Point. Like most of the Heritage Coast footpaths, this one allows the birdwatcher to spot unusual migrants with exotic residents such as oyster-catchers, avocets and marsh-harriers.*

Refer to map overleaf.

From the car park walk down to Orford quay and turn left onto the right of way which runs along the riverbank. A red and white lighthouse can be seen on the other side of the River Ore at Orford Ness. Early experiments in radar were carried out here by a team of scientists led by Sir Robert Watson-Watt, which proved vital in the early years of the Second World War.

It was the growth of the shingle bank across the mouth of the river which caused Orford's decline as a seaport in the seventeenth century. The right of way turns inland off the embankment to cross a footbridge after about half a mile. This dykeside path heads towards the village, passing a row of tall conifers to reach a road (**A**).

Turn right here by a disused sandpit which reveals interesting strata, and turn left at the rectory. Pass two lanes leading off to the left, and just after the fire station take a footpath on the left leading into the churchyard. The spacious church, dedicated to St Bartholomew and dating from 1166, is well-known for having staged the first performances of two of Benjamin Britten's most famous works — *Curlew River* and *Noye's Fludde*. It contains a magnificent fifteenth-century font as well as the parish stocks and chest.

rare landmark which looks like a headless torso. Just before the track begins to drop down turn right onto another one heading north-east (**A**). Turn right off this by an iron railing to pass a small spinney on the left. This conceals an abandoned scrapyard. The route is now heading back to Clare on another fine grassy track.

A stile on the right gives access to Clare Camp whose earthen ramparts have survived surprisingly well from late Roman times. Keep on the northern side of this common, or use the path along the hedges of its northern perimeter close to modern housing, to reach the road. Turn left and after about 300 yards (274 m) turn right (**B**) onto a concrete drive towards Hermitage Farm.

The right of way goes through the farmyard and then bears right to follow the electricity lines. Go through a gap in the hedge by the electricity poles and follow the field edge southwards. To the right is scrubland with some saplings; fallen trunks show that there was once a fine line of elms here. An unwaymarked stile on the right takes the path into woodland. It winds through the trees very pleasantly for a short way before emerging into Harps Lane beyond some disused chicken sheds. This lane leads past playing fields to meet the Cavendish road by a bridge.

Turn right to cross the bridge, and then left down an enclosed path waymarked Clare Castle Country Park, with another graveyard on the right. When the path reaches a children's play area you can fork left at this point to walk through the Country Park past the old station to return to the car park. But you are not allowed this way if you have a dog with you, in which case continue alongside the play area, past the toilets and through the white wicket gate onto a road. At the end of this short thoroughfare turn left and then left again passing the mill (now an antiques warehouse) to reach the car park entrance.

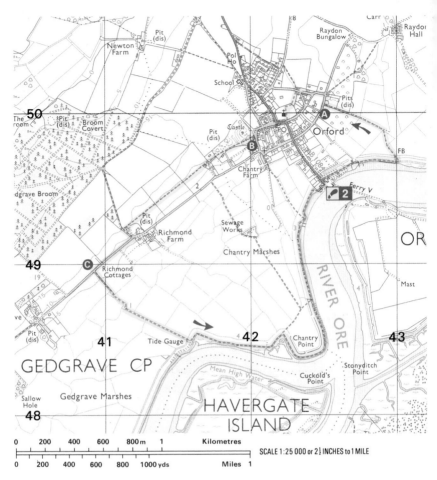

Leave the churchyard by the south gate and turn right to reach the square. A sign on the Oysterage commemorates the legendary Orford merman, caught by local fishermen in the twelfth century. Eventually, after being tortured in an attempt to make him speak, he managed to escape back to the sea and was never seen again.

Walk past the Castle Inn and through the grounds of the castle, following a track on its left side (**B**). Since this is a right of way you do not have to pay the admission charge to the castle, though of course you will should you wish to enter it. The views from the battlements are spectacular. Henry II built the castle in 1165 to a revolutionary multi-sided design. The keep is 90 feet (27 m) high and has walls ten feet (3 m) thick; although the interior is cylindrical, the exterior is much more complex, having eighteen sides. The outer defence-works are almost as impressive as the keep. Keep straight on at the footpath junction, following the sign to Gedgrave village.

This is a good path across fields; it eventually passes an asbestos barn on the left. Go down steps here to a sunken lane, turn left and, on reaching the road, right.

Walk along the road for about 400 yards (366 m) before turning left (**C**) onto a path leading through the marshes towards the river. The mudflats provide a habitat for numerous species of waders as well as other seabirds such as cormorants. The marshes support curlews whose evocative call is often heard.

At the river turn left along the raised bank. It is easy to understand East Anglian artists' love of skyscape from this viewpoint, with the village and castle small features in a landscape dominated by sky and water. Havergate Island, a bird sanctuary, is the land on the opposite side of the river as far as Chantry Point. From then the land opposite is Orford Ness, which has a famous lighthouse.

Along the riverbank footpath it seems to take little time to reach the quay at Orford, the buildings of the village coming closer all the time. Turn left up the road at the quay to return to the car park.

3 Castle Rising and the Wootton commons

Start:	Castle Rising
Distance:	5 miles (8 km)
Approximate time:	2½ hours
Parking:	Cul-de-sac to east of Castle Rising church, opposite Trinity Hospital
Refreshments:	Pubs at Castle Rising and Knights Hill
Ordnance Survey maps:	Landranger 132 (North West Norfolk) and Pathfinder 859, TF 62/72 (King's Lynn (North) & Sandringham)

General description There was an important settlement at Castle Rising long before the castle was built in 1138 — in fact

at the time of the Domesday survey there were more people than there are today. Salt-pans provided employment, as did fishing, for until 1690 the little Babingley River was tidal and it is probable that the stone used in building both the castle and church was brought here by sea. Both buildings are full of architectural interest, though the only event of real significance in the castle's history was the exile of the 'She Wolf of France', Queen Isabella, who spent twenty-seven years of comfortable semi-captivity there having abetted Mortimer in murdering her husband, Edward II, at Berkeley Castle. Much of this walk is over the lovely wild woodland of South Wootton and Ling commons.

Having inspected Castle Rising's beautiful church, and particularly the wonderful Norman west front, leave the churchyard by the eastern gate opposite Trinity Hospital (founded in 1614) and turn left along what was once the main road to Hunstanton. Pass through the gate which closes the road to traffic, and at the midpoint of the long right-hand bend (picturesquely known as Onion Corner) which runs round the northern side of Castle Rising Wood, look for a footpath on

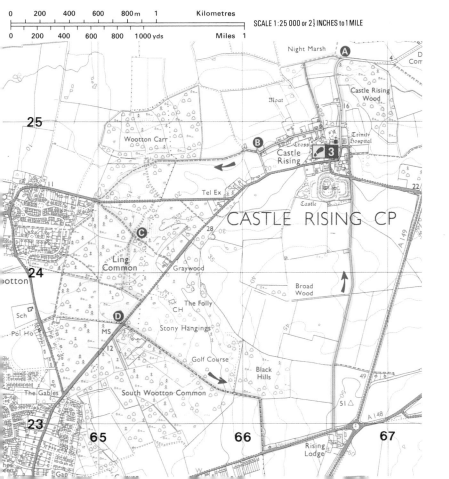

the left (**A**). Looking over the marshes it seems incredible that sailing boats once came up the river here. The ruins are of Babingley church, dedicated to St Felix, who is believed to have landed nearby in the year 600 to bring Christianity to East Anglia.

The footpath follows the edge of Night Marsh; there is a wonderful panorama towards the Sandringham woods and over the marshes. Turn left when the field-edge path meets a farm track going back to the village. Turn right when this meets a lane.

The lane leads out of the village, and where it bends sharply left take the track going straight ahead (**B**) towards a wood. Fork left by a farm building, and the track soon enters woodland known as Wootton Carr. There are some excellent Scots pines here and plenty of silver birches. Bear left away from the gamekeeper's cottage, which is built of local carrstone, and then keep straight on where the track bends to the left.

This is an excellent path through scrubland with an abundance of bracken. It soon reaches the outskirts of North Wootton. Cross the road to a waymark directly opposite (not the one by the 30 mph limit sign). After initial bogginess (mainly due to horses) this path becomes a good sandy track through the birch trees.

Almost opposite the sandpits which can be seen through the trees on the left there is a crossways. Turn right here (**C**) onto a narrow path which crosses a ditch of red water, the colour due to the iron in the local bedrock — carrstone. This path too is well-used by horses and can be very muddy at times. It leads to a ditch by a very tall pine tree, after a stunted oak standing in the middle of the track. Cross the ditch and turn left to follow it, keeping on the main sandy track to reach the road.

Turn right and after about 200 yards (183 m) take the footpath on the left (**D**) just before the property called the Black Cabin. Staggered railings have been installed on this path to make it inaccessible to riders. It strikes straight across several of the fairways of the King's Lynn golf course, but is nonetheless very pleasant walking. At the end of the golf course it bends slightly to the right and becomes a very ancient path known as Gooseberry Lane. Turn left when this reaches the main road. Fortunately there is a reasonably broad verge to walk on as the road crests the hill and then drops to the roundabout. The Knights Hill hotel here has a 'village inn'.

Turn left just before the roundabout opposite the hotel entrance onto a quiet byway which leads back to Castle Rising and gives good views of the castle. Go straight over the crossroads to reach Trinity Hospital and the church.

4 Dunwich Heath and Minsmere

Start:	Dunwich Heath
Distance:	5 miles (8 km)
Approximate time:	2 ½ hours
Parking:	Coastguard Cottages, Dunwich Heath car park (National Trust — fee payable by non-members)
Refreshments:	Pub at Eastbridge
Ordnance Survey maps:	Landranger 156 (Saxmundham & Aldeburgh) and Pathfinder 987, TM 46 (Leiston)

General description This short walk through heathland, woods and marshes is justly popular. It passes through some wonderful countryside and provides opportunities to the birdwatcher of seeing some unexpected visitors resting at Minsmere. If the weather has been at all damp, the path may be muddy in places.

Opposite the Coastguard Cottages a path leads across the heath waymarked to Eastbridge. The first few yards are part of a National Trust walk, but this soon leaves the main track and goes off to the right.

The initial stages of the walk are across sandy, heathery heathland, purpled in late summer. Keep straight on at a footpath junction to cross a stile and enter woodland. The track still winds through heather but it is more narrow now and there are silver birches and small pine trees encroaching. Fortunately they seem to have survived the strong gales of recent years rather better than the forest trees nearby.

Turn left at the next footpath junction (**A**) and continue through the wood to reach a lane which goes into the Minsmere RSPB Reserve (note that the reserve is closed on Tuesdays). Cross this lane to the bridleway opposite which has cultivated land on each side. Sizewell power station can be seen ahead. The footpath soon begins to drop down Saunders' Hill through the wind-damaged Hangman's New Wood to meet another lane into the Minsmere Reserve. Bear right here and then left at the next junction (**B**) towards Dam Bridge with its white railings. There are wide views across the marshes in both directions from here.

Almost the first building in the hamlet of Eastbridge is the Eel's Foot pub (look at its amusing sign) which is situated almost exactly at the mid-point of this walk. It serves food and Adnams ales which are a connoisseur's delight.

About 200 yards (183 m) past the Eel's Foot look for a footpath sign on the left (**C**), pointing to Minsmere Sluice. Go a few yards down this track before turning right onto a narrow path between fields. This leads to a fine viewpoint on the top of a bank fringed with gorse bushes which flower in the depths of winter. At the corner of a small wood a track leaves on the left towards a picturesque old bridge of red brick, but bear right, along the edge of the wood, at this point even though it may be muddy. The worst of the mud may be avoided alongside Sandypytle Plantation by walking on the bank of the dyke to the right of the barbed wire. This is probably the correct line of the footpath as there is an old stile at the far end. The muddy section ends at a broad drove and the going improves. The white Coastguard Cottages at the starting point can be seen to the left across Minsmere, while to the right are the ruined stone walls of an ancient chapel. In the thirteenth century, at the height of its prosperity, the merchants of Dunwich owned eighty great ships and nine churches adorned the town. Fishermen still claim to hear their bells tolling beneath the waves.

Minsmere Old River at Eastbridge

A concrete bridge takes the path to the shore at The Sluice (**D**). If it is not a Tuesday and you do not have a dog with you you may turn left and left again to walk in the Minsmere Reserve. Otherwise turn north, either on the shore or on the track behind the dunes, to return to the car park. The landward route passes birdwatching hides maintained by the RSPB overlooking the waters and reedbeds of Minsmere. Some of these are open to the public.

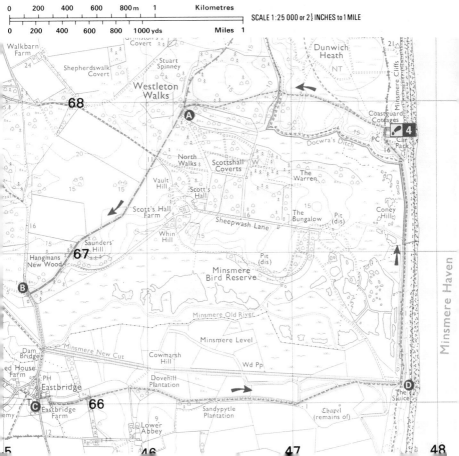

5 Constable Country

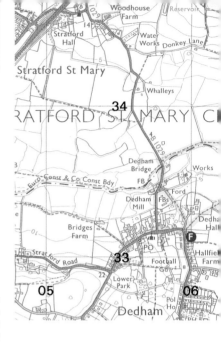

Start:	Flatford Mill, near East Bergholt
Distance:	5 miles (8 km)
Approximate time:	2½ hours
Parking:	Flatford Mill car park
Refreshments:	Pubs and tearooms at East Bergholt and Dedham
Ordnance Survey maps:	Landrangers 168 (Colchester & The Blackwater) and 169 (Ipswich & The Naze), Pathfinder 1053, TM 03/13 (Manningtree & Dedham)

General description This walk provides a leisurely way to appreciate the countryside that John Constable knew and loved. Much of the route is through beautiful meadows lined with willows, ashes and oaks whose ancestors may well have featured in some of the painter's work. Pause, if you like, to explore East Bergholt or lovely Dedham. The path back to Flatford Mill is along the banks of the Stour and is very popular.

From the car park take the clearly marked footpath to Flatford Mill. Do not cross the bridge at the bottom but bear left along the lane to Willy Lott's House. Turn left here onto the start of the Gibbonsgate Field Circular Walk, and at the end of the field turn right, following the signpost.

Take the footpath on the left (**A**) before the electricity pylon, and then walk past the pylon, keeping the hedge to the right. Cross a new stile and turn left to follow the hedge past another stile and an inviting green lane on the left (Hog's Lane) which leads towards a wood. Do not take this but keep following the fine hedge on the left: this is an ideal field path with wide views to the estuary of the Stour. Cross a double stile and continue to follow the hedge until you see cattle fencing and a gateway on the left (**B**). If the gate is closed cross the stile and plank bridge onto Dazeley's Lane, which goes to East Bergholt. A little way up the green lane there is an opening on the right which is another excellent viewpoint.

At the road turn left, and then after 50 yards (46 m) left again (**C**) onto a very narrow path with gardens on each side. (If you wish to explore East Bergholt, you can instead continue along the road to the village and then take the Flatford Road to rejoin the route at (**D**)).

The short path between the gardens continues across a field to a signpost to the right of the trees opposite. Go through this copse and along the narrow path beyond heading towards houses. Cross Hog's Lane and follow the edge of two fields to reach Clapper Farm. Descend the drive 25 yards (23 m) to a ladder-stile and climb this and cross the paddock to another stile. Turn left to reach Flatford Road (**D**) and go straight across onto another narrow field-edge path. This leads to a planting of young trees which discreetly veils a sewage works. Two more new stiles take the path across a loke and into a field. Cross this to yet another new stile which gives onto a lane. Again this is crossed directly to a gate of black-painted metal with stile attached. From here there is a classic view of Dedham Vale. Dedham church is to the left, that of Stratford St Mary to the right.

Cross the lovely meadow to a bridge at the bottom (**E**) and follow the track for 100 yards (91 m) to where the track divides by a clump of willows. Fork right away from Fen Bridge onto a shady path beneath the arched branches of the hedging trees. At the end of this path a stile gives access to a broad river meadow. The path soon reaches the riverbank and follows it to Dedham Bridge.

Cross the bridge. If you wish to visit the village with its beautiful church (Dedham is connected with another famous East Anglian artist, Sir Alfred Munnings) follow the road. If you would rather continue along footpaths turn left off the road opposite the mill — which is now luxury flats — to cross the river by a footbridge. Immediately after the crossing take the footpath on the right. This

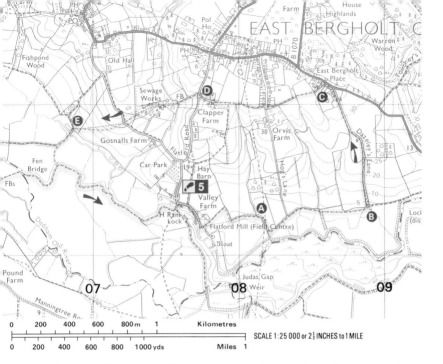

skirts a field and then the garden and duckpond of Dedham Hall to reach Muniment House (**F**) where those who explored Dedham would rejoin the route.

The return leg of the walk begins to the left of Muniment House where a gate opens onto a field track which passes behind Dedham Hall. Bear to the right away from the farmyard to reach a stile and a pathway leading down towards the river. This crosses a footbridge over the course of the old river and heads towards the riverbank which it reaches by a fine willow tree. Turn right to follow the winding course of the Stour to Flatford Mill, crossing the bridge there to return to the car park.

Willy Lott's House, Flatford Mill

6 Bungay, Bath Hills and the Bigod Way

Start:	Bungay
Distance:	5 miles (8 km)
Approximate time:	3 hours
Parking:	Priory Lane car park in Bungay town centre
Refreshments:	Pub at Earsham, pubs and cafés at Bungay
Ordnance survey maps:	Landranger 156 (Saxmundham & Aldeburgh), Pathfinders 924, TM 29/39 (Loddon & Hempnall) and 945, TM 28/38 (Bungay & Harleston)

General description *The River Waveney is the boundary between Norfolk and Suffolk for much of its course, and its upper reaches flow through and enhance some of the loveliest countryside of the two counties. This short walk allows appreciation of this, both from the top of the valley at Ditchingham, and from the side of the river itself, on the return leg from Earsham. The gravel pits at Earsham, passed on the walk, are a breeding site of the great crested grebe whose courtship display (including the presentation of love tokens — usually strands of waterweed — by male to female) is one of the most remarkable of the bird world.*

Bungay is a delightful small market town, with a wonderful treasury of ancient buildings, including a massive castle built by the Bigods — from whom a local footpath takes its name — and the opportunity of exploring the town should be taken.

From the car park follow Priory Lane round to Castle Orchard and then take the bridleway on the left which runs in front of the castle. The remains standing today are those of the castle built *c.*1300 by the last of the earls of Bigod. Earlier this family had received vast estates in East Anglia as a reward for the support that they gave William the Conqueror. The original castle dated from the time of the Conqueror, but in 1174 the Bigods fell foul of King Henry II and the castle was demolished. After the death of the last Earl Bigod in 1307 the stronghold reverted to the Crown. The Bigod Way, a network of paths around Bungay initiated by the town council, begins at the castle, and this route follows one of these paths. A picnic area occupies the castle's outer bailey and gives wide views over the water meadows.

Near Roaring Arch Bridge, Bungay

The bridleway that passes in front of the castle leads to a footpath which emerges in the yard of the White Lion Inn. Walk through this to Earsham Street and turn left to pass the post office and then right into Outney Road. This ends at a footbridge across the bypass. Cross the bridge onto Outney Common and turn right onto the track leading from the golf clubhouse to join a footpath which runs on the far side of the pond by the roundabout.

The path leaves the common through a kissing-gate onto marshes. This is a part of the Bigod Way associated with George Baldry whose book *The Rabbit Skin Hat* is a classic of country lore. It is a lovely path across marshland pasture.

At the riverbank bear right to the narrow iron footbridges which take the path into Norfolk: the first bridge is over the 'old' river — the Waveney now takes a wide sweep. As the path emerges from the trees there is a footpath junction (**A**). Turn left here, continuing to follow the Bigod Way, and pass through a kissing-gate into a meadow. The drive to Ditchingham Lodge runs through this meadow, and on the other side the path climbs up a steep hill.

From the summit there are lovely tree-fringed views over the Waveney. The path continues westwards along the top of the valley, with brambles making it narrow at times. It passes underneath a private wooden footbridge and here it may become quite boggy in wet weather. A little further on logs are thoughtfully provided as seats at a viewpoint.

At Bath Hills (**B**) the path joins a farm drive and begins its descent. These south-facing slopes were covered with vineyards in Roman and Norman times. Bath Hills Farm was originally Bath House. A cold spring here was promoted as health-enhancing in 1730 and Bungay achieved brief fame as a spa town — many years before Bath or Cheltenham.

The route runs through a pleasant wood after Bath House (though this screens views of the river) and then passes through a gate — there is an old ice house on the right. It climbs above Valley House and then drops to join its driveway. There are lovely views over grazing marshes from here, and the rare stinking iris likes this habitat. Beyond Valley Farm the road is metalled. It is a lovely winding lane through woods at first but further on there are gravel workings, although the ponds left from previous workings are enjoyed by a variety of waterbirds. Beware of fast-moving lorries along this lane.

At the road junction bear left to Earsham and cross the main road to a footpath on the other side leading into a blocked-off road. Pass the post office and the pub and cross the road — the famous Otter Trust is about a mile along it to the right — to a footpath to the left of the war memorial and village hall.

The footpath leads across a common towards the church. Turn left at the lane and pass the church, which is often locked, to cross a hump-backed bridge (**C**). Another branch of the Bigod Way, now joined with the Angles Way, goes off to the right here, but continue ahead.

The track becomes a path which leads down to cross a small river, a diversion from the Waveney, by a footbridge (**D**). Turn left along the riverbank, and it is a lovely stroll back to Bungay from here. The small river teems with fish and other wildlife. To the right beyond the main river the town is dominated by the twin towers of the castle. At the road turn right at Roaring Arch Bridge and then, having crossed another bridge, take the first turn right into Castle Lane. The left fork into Castle Orchard leads to Priory Lane and so to the car park.

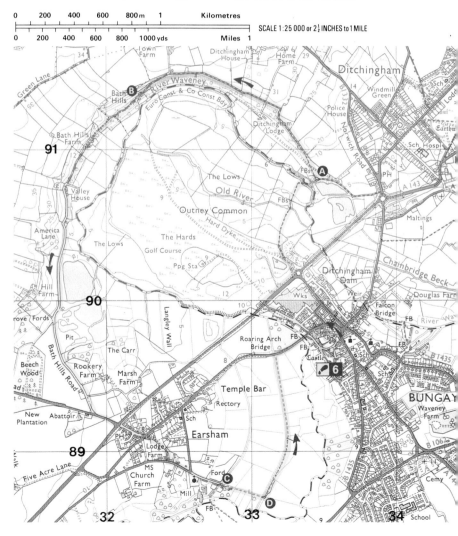

SCALE 1:25 000 or 2½ INCHES to 1 MILE

7 Lavenham and Brent Eleigh

Start:	Lavenham
Distance:	5 miles (8 km)
Approximate time:	2½ hours
Parking:	Church Street car park at Lavenham
Refreshments:	Pubs and tea rooms at Lavenham, pub at Brent Eleigh
Ordnance Survey maps:	Landranger 155 (Bury St Edmunds & Sudbury) and Pathfinder 1029, TL 84/94 (Sudbury & Lavenham)

General description *The medieval prosperity of Lavenham, founded on the woollen trade, is reflected in a wealth of beautiful timber-framed buildings. The church was built with money from the same trade. Its tower, 141 feet (43 m) high, may seem out of balance with the nave and chancel, though inside the main impression is one of airy space. The bells are among the most famous in England, the tenor reputedly having the finest tone of any bell to be found in the country. In contrast, the little church of*

Brent Eleigh, visited on the walk, retains its box pews and medieval wall paintings. It is a highlight of a lovely walk through quiet, beautiful countryside. Some of the paths and tracks are likely to be muddy except in the driest summer weather.

Leave the car park, which is just to the east of Lavenham church, and turn right into Church Street. Turn right again into Bear's Lane, which leads past the housing development of Meadow Close. Keep to the lane, ignoring a footpath going to the right, to pass the half-thatched, half-pantiled Mill Cottage. After Weaners Farm and immediately before Bear's Lane Farm take the footpath on the left (**A**), which skirts around the farm buildings, to reach a pond. Turn left again here onto a field-edge track.

Keep straight on at a footpath junction, past a 'No Horses' notice, which is not always heeded. Unusually for this county, there are excellent hedges here. Turn right at the end of a long field; the broad track snakes down, very churned up by hooves.

At a footpath junction by a group of oak trees (**B**) keep straight on to leave the track used by horses. There is now a ditch on the left and beyond it a spinney of young poplars. The walking is at its best here on a grassy path on the edge of the field.

The path threads its way through a recent planting of new trees, mostly poplars though there are also oak, beech and birch. Yellow

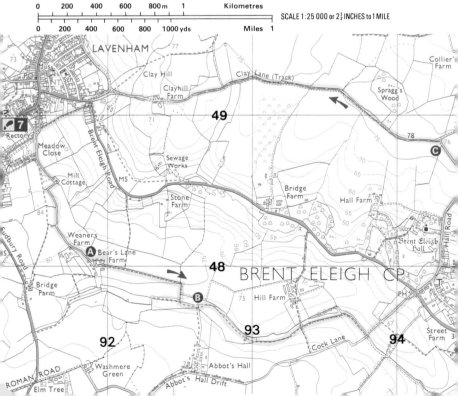

Lavenham, a Suffolk wool town

8 Walberswick marshes and common

Start:	Walberswick
Distance:	5 miles (8 km)
Approximate time:	2 hours
Parking:	Ferry Road car park at Walberswick
Refreshments:	Pubs at Walberswick
Ordnance Survey maps:	Landranger 156 (Saxmundham & Aldeburgh) and Pathfinder 966, TM 47/57 (Southwold & Halesworth)

General description *Bracing sea breezes may well be the most memorable feature of this walk, though the return is inland through salt marshes and reedbed to heathland, where the path uses a section of the trackbed of the old Halesworth to Southwold railway, closed many years ago. Birdwatchers will particularly enjoy the path through the marshes, the home or resting place of many interesting species, including marsh and hen harriers and bearded tits.*

Refer to map overleaf.

Follow the River Blyth seaward from the Ferry Road car park and turn southwards on reaching the shore. Although the beach at Walberswick is mainly of stone and shingle there is usually some smooth sand to walk on. A great bank of sand has been bulldozed into place between shore and marsh to act as a sea defence. The Dunwich River – which was crossed by footbridge soon after the start of the walk – flows through the marshes a little way inland from the bank.

The tower of St Andrew's Church can be seen dominating the village of Walberswick. Much of this church was pulled down when the prosperity of the village declined in the seventeenth century. Ahead lies Dunwich, hardly a village now but in medieval times a busy seaport with 5,000 inhabitants. In 1326 much of the town was swept away over-night by a terrible storm which also blocked off its harbour.

Turn inland (**A**) from the shore when nearly opposite Dingle Great Hill, a tongue of land striking into the marshes. The path follows the left bank of a creek, heading towards a sail-less windmill – since it crosses part of the nature reserve dogs should be on leads. The reeds here are a valuable crop, harvested by machinery. Much more enduring than

arrows fixed to the young trees show the right of way. Turn right and then immediately left to cross the concrete driveway which goes to the lovely, rambling Hill Farm. The path runs along the edge of another field with a thick hedge on the left. After a little way this thins to allow a view of a lake. The tower of Brent Eleigh church can be seen beyond.

Turn left at Cock Lane, which climbs steeply. Pause at the gate at the crest of the hill to enjoy the view of Brent Eleigh Hall, restyled by Lutyens in 1933, and the church. The lane then descends to the road by the thatched pub.

Cross the road and follow the lane towards the church – the village, of scattered cottages, lies on the byway to the right. St Mary's Church is one of the gems of Suffolk. It has an excellent guidebook, by Canon Fitch, which not only throws light on the history of this church but explains how various aesthetic, social and liturgical factors wrought change on churches throughout the land at various periods. The most celebrated features of the church are the medieval wall paintings on the east wall, its box pews dating from the seventeenth century, and the baroque monument to Edward Colman.

Continue along the road and bear left where it forks. There are fine views from this hilltop, with three church towers to be seen, not counting that of St Mary's which is hidden by trees. When the road bears sharply to the right take the track on the left (**C**) which leads westwards towards Lavenham. This is Clay Lane, aptly named in times of wet weather as it is a bridleway well used by horses.

The track winds through ancient hedgerows for more than 1 mile (1.5 km) before reaching a metalled lane near Clayhill Farm. The riding stables are situated close by. Descend to reach the Brent Eleigh road, and turn left along it for about 25 yards (23 m). By a three-storey brick terrace of houses turn right on a waymarked field-edge footpath which leads to Bear's Lane opposite the new development of Meadow Close. Turn right here, and then left into Church Street to return to the start.

SCALE 1:25 000 or 2½ INCHES to 1 MILE

straw thatch, roofs made of Suffolk reed are to be found all over southern England.

The path joins with another near the windmill after crossing the Dunwich River; bear right here. This path comes from Newdelight Walks, about three miles inland, and is a wonderful right of way passing through marshy woodland and a vast reedbed. This is certainly a difficult path for twitchers to resist when there are such rarities as the bittern, with its unmistakable booming call, living here. Turn left at the next footpath junction (**B**), leaving the bank of the river to head across the marsh towards East Hill.

A very short climb takes the path from reedbed to heathland and onto a sandy track which threads through clumps of broom, gorse and bramble to reach a road. Cross this and bear slightly left to cross East Sheep

Walk and reach a shelter belt of Scots pines and birches. Near the end of this, fork right towards Eastwoodlodge Farm and join the main road. Turn right and pass the farm, and then turn left (**C**) off the road through a farm gate into a meadow. The path runs parallel to the old Southwold & Halesworth Light Railway track, heading towards the town, with the water tower and lighthouses as distinctive landmarks. This railway had a charming eccentricity, which may have been partly due to its rolling stock which had been built for the Emperor of China but was never delivered. The outlines of imperial dragons were dimly visible under the Southwold & Halesworth paintwork.

The footpath passes through an old cutting of the railway, its heather much appreciated by the rabbits. It becomes very busy with walkers as it approaches the bridge at Southwold Harbour. Do not cross this but turn right onto the interesting riverbank path past a host of small boats tied to rickety-looking stagings. The inhabitants of Walberswick used to be known as 'Walberswick Whisperers' because of their loud voices − a consequence of their having to shout across great expanses of reedy marshland. In the summer a ferry operates across the river to Southwold from a staging at the end of the riverside path, which returns to the starting point.

9 Castle Acre and the River Nar valley

Start:	Castle Acre
Distance:	6 miles (9.5 km)
Approximate time:	3 hours
Parking:	Roadside parking at Castle Acre village green
Refreshments:	Pubs at Castle Acre and at West Acre (no food at latter)
Ordnance Survey maps:	Landranger 132 (North West Norfolk) and Pathfinders 880, TF 61/71 (King's Lynn (South)) and 881, TF 81/91 (East Dereham & Castle Acre)

General description *This is an undemanding route across countryside that is reminiscent of the Cotswolds, with gentle hills enfolding villages hidden among trees and a sparkling river which is deliciously refreshing to the feet on a hot day. Castle Acre has notable historical monuments in the remains of its lovely priory and Norman castle, the latter sited on top of a very well-preserved motte.*

From the village green in Castle Acre walk towards the church and the priory ruins, passing the former on your left. At the entrance to the priory car park turn right and then take the track to the left at End House. The lovely rolling landscape typical of this walk is immediately apparent. The track winds down a hill towards a wood and a pond, both on the left. After the pond turn off the track onto a path on the left (**A**) which may be damp after wet weather.

The path winds on through tall willow-herb, which is usually kept in check by cutting. It approaches woods with fine willows around the edge and enters these over a stile. The excellent walking continues on the path through the woods.

A gate at the end of the woodland leads into a meadow used for horse-jumping practice. Head for the gap in the trees ahead to find a stile followed by two footbridges; the mill is on the left. When you come to the lane (**B**) turn left and then right onto a pleasant sandy track which leads to another ford; before reaching the ford look for a hedgerow on the left (**C**), from where a field-edge path heads south. If you wish to visit West Acre continue past the ford to reach the village and the Stag, an old-fashioned village inn which doesn't serve food.

From (**C**) take the field-edge path south and cross over the road onto a track which runs along the right-hand edge of a field towards a pylon, its alien features marring a lovely landscape. The track passes a wood on

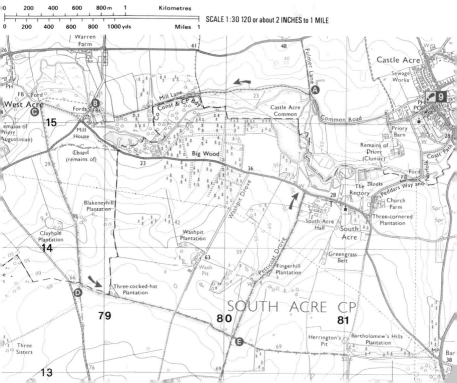

The ruins of Castle Acre Priory

Start:	Honing Common, 3 miles (4·75 km) south-east of North Walsham
Distance:	6½ miles (10·5 km). Shorter version 4 miles (6·5 km)
Approximate time:	2½ hours (1½ hours for shorter version)
Parking:	Off the road at Honing Common
Refreshments:	Pubs near the route at Dilham, Honing and East Ruston
Ordnance Survey maps:	Landrangers 133 (North East Norfolk) and 134 (Norwich & The Broads), Pathfinder 862, TG 22/32 (Norfolk Broads (North))

the left and climbs gradually up a long hill. At the top (**D**) where the track goes to the right leave it by turning left at a blue waymark, following the hedge, which is on your right, towards a clump of trees picturesquely called Three-cocked-hat Plantation. Move to the field on your right at this point and walk with the hedge on the left.

Cross straight over Washpit Drove to the track on the other side. There are wide vistas from here over the west Norfolk countryside. Turn left at the next track which crosses (**E**), which has the charming name of Petticoat Drove. The tiny cottage on the edge of the woods below has an equally pleasing name – Fingerhill Cottage. There is a wide view over the valley as the track drops down. Petticoat Drove reaches the lane into South Acre passing the hall, a fine building surrounded by paddocks. Turn right to reach tiny South Acre church which contains an astonishing amount of history (it is under the care of English Heritage). The north chapel is the oldest part of the church and contains the richly decorated monument to Sir Edward Barkham, who was Lord Mayor of London in the early seventeenth century. At its centre is a macabre panel of a heap of skulls. At the entrance to the chapel there is an effigy of a crusader, a Knight Templar who could have been Sir Eudo Harsyke who died in the twelfth century.

After the church bear left when the lane divides to drop down to the River Nar, which is crossed by a footbridge. This beauty spot offers another excellent opportunity to refresh tired feet.

Continue up the lane; it leads behind Castle Acre church directly to the priory car park. If you wish to reach the centre of the village turn right into Blind Street and then left onto the main road, passing through the ancient gateway onto the village green.

General description *The Weavers Way is a 56-mile (90 km) walk along footpaths, a disused railway track and country lanes between Cromer and Great Yarmouth. The delightful short stretch of the Weavers Way in this walk is typical of much of the remainder. The longest part is on the bank of the North Walsham to Dilham canal, a waterway which was built in 1824 and fell into disuse about a hundred years later. This countryside is in a forgotten corner of the Broads, far away from the busy rivers. It is a reminder of how quiet it must have been in bygone days when wind and horse power were the chief means of moving traffic.*

From Honing Common walk to the railway bridge which took the road between Dilham and Honing over the Midland & Great Northern line between King's Lynn and Great Yarmouth. Go down the short track on the right-hand side of this splendid steel bridge (note the decorative clover leaves) and turn left onto the Weavers Way, which uses the abandoned trackbed at this point.

At first the walking is through woodland, and this gives way to open farmland with wide views on either side. The line saw its last train more than thirty years ago but granite ballast remains underfoot to chastise those walking in trainers.

Oak trees of surprising height, considering their youth, are encroaching on the track. A small bridge takes the track over a very murky dyke and it then passes through a gate. Turn off the Weavers Way before a second gate, where a notice points the way to the

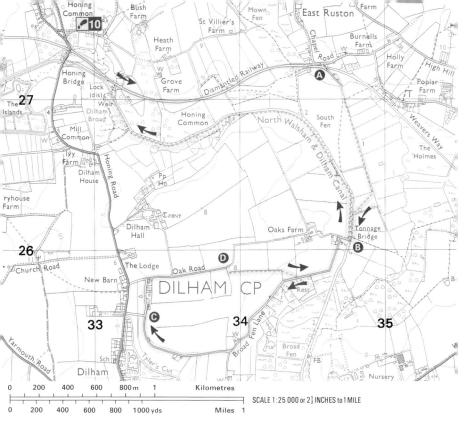

Butchers Arms at East Ruston, which is just under 1 mile (1·5 km) from this point.

Turn right here (**A**) onto a farm track, heading for the marshes. A crossing-keeper used to live in the flint cottage here; his duties could never have been very demanding. The crossing-gates serve to keep the cattle in the meadow on the right. This 40-acre field was in earlier times part of the common land of East Ruston. Take the track leading down its eastern side. After a second gate cross a field diagonally to reach Tonnage Bridge (**B**), a beautiful brick bridge which spans the North Walsham & Dilham Canal. The bridge was restored in 1982 at a cost of £32,000. Cross the bridge.

If you wish to do only the shorter version of the walk, turn immediately right along the tow path, following the route after (B) below.

Turn left just past the cottage onto Broad Fen Lane. This makes excellent walking. At first there is wild woodland on the left, then the lane reaches open countryside and becomes less muddy, more of a green way. Beyond Keeper's Cottage it is a quiet country lane which curves northwards to reach the short road (**C**) leading down to Dilham Staithe, the head of navigation. This road also leads to the village and pub — turn left at the main road to explore these. Otherwise keep straight on along the lane, past the road

to the staithe, to reach Oak Road. Turn right onto this at Holly Cottage, which has a striking weather vane, and walk eastwards as far as the start of the driveway to Oaks Farm, where brick pillars announce the start of the private road (**D**).

Turn right here and then immediately left onto a waymarked path along the right-hand edge of a field, with a well-kept thorn hedge to the right. Turn left when this path meets Broad Fen Lane again, and walk back to Tonnage Bridge (**B**).

Take the footpath on the left immediately before the bridge onto the west bank of the canal. This quiet stretch of deserted waterway is a haven for many rare birds, including kingfishers. It provides a wide range of habitats — coniferous and broad-leaved woodland, marsh, meadowland and reedbed. There is a fine new footbridge over a dyke towards the end of this stretch. Dilham Broad once occupied the site of the meadow here.

The sound of rushing water is heard in the last woodland glade. This heralds Honing Lock, where there was once a lock-keeper's cottage. The lock-keeper must have enjoyed a tranquil life here: the canal was so short of water that only three wherries could use it each day. Cross the bridge over the lock and follow the footpath up to rejoin the Weavers Way. Turn left to return to Honing Common.

11 The Raynhams

Start:	West Raynham
Distance:	5½ miles (8·75 km)
Approximate time:	2½ hours
Parking:	West Raynham — park on right-hand side of Greyhound Inn car park near bottle-bank
Refreshments:	Pub at West Raynham
Ordnance Survey maps:	Landranger 132 (North West Norfolk) and Pathfinder 860, TF 82/92 (The Raynhams & Fakenham (South))

General description *This walk is a variation of the one promoted by the village and available as a pamphlet. Raynham Hall, built in 1630, is the seat of the Townshend family, whose most notable member was the 2nd Viscount 'Turnip' Townshend, who revolutionised farming with the introduction of his ideas on the rotation of crops. The house is not open to the public, but its exterior is well seen from points on this walk, especially from the lovely churchyard which is situated within the park. St Martin's Church at South Raynham — an isolated little building containing a unique stone* mensa, *a holy table dating from the thirteenth century — is also passed on the route.*

Turn right out of the Greyhound Inn car park and bear right again at the road junction, following the Helhoughton road. After 200 yards (183 m) look for a finger-post footpath sign on the right pointing towards a playing field. Follow the path along the edge of the field to the playing field, cross this to the right-hand side of Round Plantation and follow the path round to a stile (**A**). Turn right, following the green circular-walk badge.

The broad, grassy track follows the edge of the field to a gale-damaged wood on the left. On the right is the embankment of the lake, of which tantalising glimpses may be seen.

After crossing the stream go through a kissing-gate and turn right towards the farm. Raynham Hall can be seen on the left, although the view is a little marred by the unsightly water tower.

In Victorian times Raynham was held to be the third grandest of the stately homes of the county. It was built for Sir Roger Townshend in 1630, probably from designs by Inigo Jones. Charles, the 2nd Viscount, 'Turnip' Townshend, succeeded to the title in 1697. 'To this nobleman, the kingdom is indebted for the general cultivation of *turnips,* which

Winter walking near South Raynham

had previously been grown only in gardens; but observing their advantages while in attendance upon George I, at Hanover, he brought the seed and practice into England', a Victorian writer explained. Pass through the farm- and stable-yard to reach the church, which dates from 1868, pausing *en route* for a fine view down the main drive to Raynham Hall.

Leave the park and turn left onto the road to pass the gate-lodge (**B**). Turn left again immediately to follow the field edge eastwards, keeping a fence on the left. There are further views of the hall from here. At the wood — where there is a fine display of snowdrops in early spring — bear right and follow along the edge of it to a shrubbery of laurels. The wall of the walled garden can be seen ahead. The path joins with a track winding through the laurels. Bear left onto this, keeping the walled garden to the right. The track goes close to the main drive to the hall but is discreetly screened by the laurels. There is a paddock on the right. Eventually the track joins with the drive at the gate-lodge. Turn right onto the main road.

Before the telephone-box turn left onto the lane to Colkirk, a little-used byway which is now hedgeless but in compensation gives wide views over the countryside.

The lane dips down to a slight right-hand bend and then climbs to a sharper left-hand corner. Turn right here (**C**) onto the track which runs along the crest of the hill. At Corn Bill Coppice — an interesting memorial to parliamentary history — a concessionary path joins from the left. Keep to the main track, which makes excellent walking, to reach Webb's Covert, a dark planting of conifers on the left. Another bridleway joins from the right but our route keeps on to pass Norman's Burrow House, a remote cottage, on the left. After this there is a stream on the left, and then a great series of pits which must have given the place its name of Norman's Burrow. Presumably sand and gravel were once extracted from this hillside.

Turn right at the road and follow this to South Raynham. Turn left onto the main road here, and just before the petrol station turn right (**D**) onto a footpath which goes through a low meadow, heading towards the church. Cross the footbridge at the end of the field into another meadow and in this pass over two plank bridges to reach a stile. Head across the next field towards the white gates of the large house which was once the rectory. Turn right onto the track which goes past the church.

St Martin's Church at South Raynham is a fourteenth-century building famous for its stone *mensa*, or communion table, which is at least a century earlier. Most similar items of church furniture were destroyed during the Reformation, but this one was hidden and then used as a paving slab for many centuries before being rediscovered and restored to its original function.

Continue along the track through a gate leading into another low meadow. Cross this diagonally to a gate in the far right corner (the first gate you see is like a false summit, but head for this anyway and then go over a plank bridge to reach the corner of the field). Now follow the stream – the infant River Wensum lies just beyond this – for some distance, before in the last field bearing left to climb to a stile onto the road. Turn left here and at the village bear right towards the telephone-box. Pass West Raynham post office and the ivy-clad remains of St Margaret's Church, which was abandoned after 1780, before reaching the Greyhound Inn.

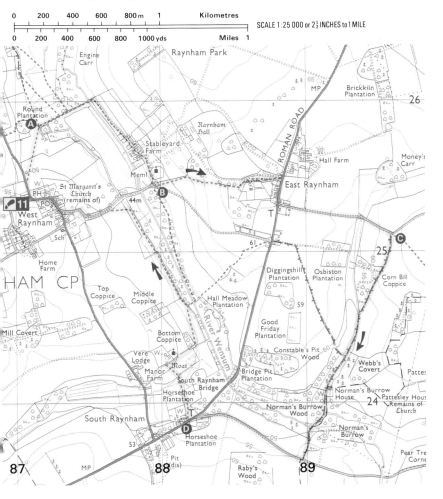

SCALE 1:25 000 or 2½ INCHES to 1 MILE

12 Hoxne –
St Edmund's
village

Start:	Hoxne
Distance:	7 miles (11·25 km)
Approximate time:	3 ½ hours
Parking:	Limited street parking in Hoxne
Refreshments:	Pubs at Hoxne and Billingford
Ordnance Survey maps:	Landranger 156 (Saxmundham & Aldeburgh), Pathfinders 964, 07/17 (Diss (South) & Botesdale) and 944, TM 0818 (Diss (North) & Kenninghall)

General description *Half of this walk is in Norfolk and half in Suffolk, the River Waveney being the boundary between the two counties. The walk is on lanes and field paths through the country that King Edmund, East Anglia's martyred saint, must have known. He was killed by the Danes near Hoxne in 869 and his body (having been miraculously reunited with its head, which the Danes had cut off) was buried close by. Nearly 200 years later it was moved to Bury St Edmunds where a shrine was established by King Canute in the abbey church.*

Walk up Hoxne street, forking right at the Green, which has a roofed shelter, and continue towards the church. Cross the road to visit it – there are medieval wall-paintings high on the nave wall and an interesting exhibition of antiquities and bygones in the north aisle. Turn left from the churchyard onto the B1118.

Just beyond Church Close turn left (**A**) down Water Mill Lane. The round-towered church at Thorpe Abbots can be seen ahead as the lane divides; bear left down to the river and cross it by the bridge. A new cut takes the main flow of water, isolating this meander which is left stagnant and weed-choked. Turn left after the bridge to follow the river to another bridge over the new cut where the water rushes over the weir. Turn left after this bridge too and follow the riverbank to a small wood (**B**). Cross the stile that faces you here and then turn sharply right, passing an Angles Way sign and following the edge of the field with the fence on the right.

There is a post bearing a waymark in front of the next clump of trees. Cross the plank

bridge here and follow the left side of the wood. When this ends there is a lovely view to the right over marshes. Now follow the hedge on the right. When the path meets a farm track cross it to the stile opposite (the Angles Way goes off to the right here).

You are now in a narrow, green way which climbs to the main road. Cross to the lane to Thorpe Abbots which is almost opposite. Walk down the lane towards the village, passing School Lane on the left. At Highfield Trout Fishery (**C**) turn left down the drive and follow the track round to the right to the car park. Turn left here, by the fly-fishing pond, to walk below the embankment to a plank bridge. Cross this to a field-edge path leading towards a red-brick house called Wood Cottage. Pass behind the cottage and turn left and then almost immediately right onto a sandy track which winds invitingly towards woodland.

Bear left at a narrow planting of conifers (**D**) and follow the right-hand edge of these. Turn right at the bottom and walk on the field edge with the hedge on the left. Just before the next clump of woodland study the ditch on the left carefully to find and cross a perilous plank bridge overgrown with vegetation. Cross the field facing you diagonally to the back drive to Grove Farm, and at the drive turn left to the farmhouse, skirting round it to the right to reach a lane.

Turn left onto the lane and then fork right to pass a telephone-box. The surface of this byway varies from tarmac to concrete and then to hard-core as it passes several delightful cottages. The lane bears sharply left (**E**) to pass the last of these. It now becomes a lovely green way.

Fork left when this divides to pass the site of two cottages which are marked on the map but no longer in evidence. The track now approaches Hall Farm where the right of way passes through the farmyard, turns left and then immediately right to reach the driveway passing Billingford church. This is usually locked, although the key is available. There is a lovely view over the Waveney valley from the churchyard, with Billingford Mill and Scole church notable landmarks. Turn right at the main road (**F**), and then left by the Horseshoes pub.

From the mill a footpath winds its way over the common to the bridge where there is a tranquil pastoral scene of water and meadows. After crossing the river turn right into Oakley and then left in the village onto the road to Brome.

Pass Hill View Cottage and at the next corner, before Oakley House, turn left down a farm road marked 'Private' (**G**). Bear right where the drive splits into three, following the waymarks, and then bear left to pass The Lodge whose Tudor-style chimneys can be

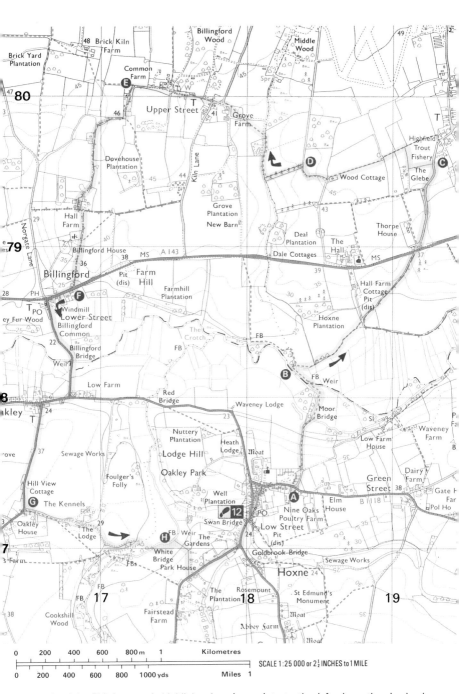

SCALE 1:25 000 or 2½ INCHES to 1 MILE

seen to the right. This is a scenic highlight of the walk, with the path dropping to the river again. At the bottom the drive sheers right to pass by small brick pillars, but the footpath follows the fence on the left. It crosses White Bridge, a delightfully decayed structure with many of its cast-iron railings missing. Hoxne church can be seen on the left. A footpath sign points to the left along the riverbank after the bridge; follow the direction of this and when a fence blocks further progress by the river, at the end of the plantation, turn right along the field edge (**H**). This path leads up to the road, past a large modern house of red brick. Turn left onto the road to return to Hoxne.

13 River Waveney walk

Start:	Beccles
Distance:	7 ½ miles (12 km)
Approximate time:	3 hours
Parking:	Beccles Quay car park
Refreshments:	Pubs at Beccles and Geldeston
Ordnance Survey maps:	Landrangers 134 (Norwich & The Broads) and 156 (Saxmundham & Aldeburgh), Pathfinders 924, TM 29/39 (Loddon & Hempnall), 925, TM 49/59 (Lowestoft & Beccles (North)), and 946, TM 48/58 (Beccles (South))

General description The head of navigation on the River Waveney is at Geldeston Locks and the stretch upriver from Beccles is one of the few under-used stretches of Broadland waterway, even in high summer. The valley of the Waveney here remains grazing land and from the riverbank there are wide views across the marshes, with the opportunity of seeing wetland birds and plants. The return route is mainly on a lonely sandy track crossing rolling fields.

From the Broads Authority Information Centre on the quay at Beccles walk back towards the town past the Loaves and Fishes pub. Turn right at the end of Fen Lane and cross the bridge over the River Waveney. Turn immediately left (**A**) following a finger-post sign down some steps onto the river flood-wall. Follow this through the boatyard and past the piles of timber. There is a waymark on the pier of the old railway bridge (LNER 1938) and soon afterwards the track ends and the right of way becomes a narrow riverbank footpath pleasantly fringed by rosebay willow-herb. On the opposite bank a fine array of houses of various periods makes a striking foreground for the large parish church, which can be visited later. Nearly opposite the swimming pool the path mounts to the top of the river embankment, which it follows for most of the way to Geldeston.

The riverbank path goes through the small patch of carr woodland at Dunburgh Hill and on to Geldeston Dyke. This cut brought the river to the village and was important commercially in the days when wherries were

the chief means of transport. Go under the old railway bridge and through the boatyard to reach the village. At The Street turn left to pass, or pause at, the Wherry pub. The crinkle-crankle wall here was designed to cut down the reverberation of clattering horse-drawn traffic and is a feature often found in East Anglian villages. Turn left towards Ellingham at the main road.

Pass the disused station on the right and where the road bends to the right turn left (**B**), following a signboard, on the track over the marshes to the Locks Inn. Thirty years ago this was the loneliest of Broadland pubs, kept by an elderly lady from Edinburgh, Miss Susan Ellis. There was no electricity at the Locks then and no road reached it. Miss Ellis often had to be rescued by the water bailiff in winter when the flood level rose to the upper floors of the building. She was not in favour of ladies drinking and would ration them to one bottle of beer (there was no draught) unless they were particular favourites. Memories of the romantic oil-lit pub in those days linger, and it is interesting to think what Miss Ellis's comments might be if she could see the greatly enlarged pub today.

The Locks takes its name from Ship-meadow Lock which was the first of the three locks which took the navigation up to Bungay until 1934. Turn to the right before the pub to cross the bridge over the dyke and then follow it to the bridges over the lock, the old river, and the New Cut.

Cross the three bridges and carry straight on across the marsh with the dyke on the right. Beyond a massive sprawling willow go through a gate onto a track and turn right. After the waterworks this becomes a made-up lane. Just before it reaches the sewage works look for a stile on the left (**C**) with an Angles Way sign. Climb this, keep the fence on the right to another stile in the corner of the field, and then a third stile takes the path straight across the next field. Walk along the edge of a wood that is sadly depleted of trees. The tower of Beccles church can be seen ahead. Pass the driveway to Barsham Hall, opposite some cottages, keeping straight on along the sandy track. You may be fortunate enough to see a kingfisher where this crosses Barsham Dyke: there are usually plenty of fish to be glimpsed from the bridge.

The River Waveney at Beccles

The pleasant track eventually joins the main road before Roos Hall — there is a good footpath which initially keeps the route away from the highway. The gaunt red-brick hall is supposed to be haunted by a coach and four with a headless driver on Christmas Eve.

After the hall turn to the left down Puddingmoor to Beccles. If you wish to see the church look for steps on the right. At the Market Place turn left onto Northgate, which has a wonderful succession of old buildings, grand and humble. At the end of Northgate carry straight on into Bridge Street which takes you back to the quay.

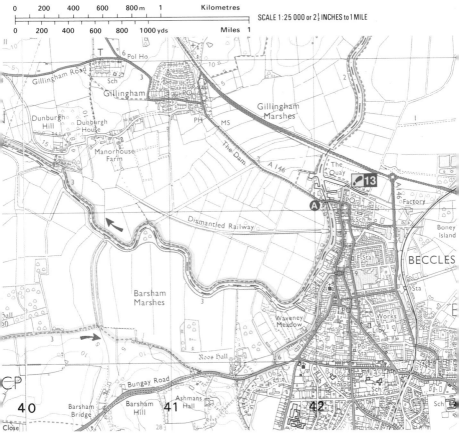

14 The Tattingstone Wonder and Stutton Ness

Start:	Stutton
Distance:	7½ miles (12 km)
Approximate time:	2½ hours
Parking:	Alton Water car park at Stutton
Refreshments:	Pubs at Stutton
Ordnance Survey maps:	Landrangers 168 (Colchester & The Blackwater) and 169 (Ipswich & The Naze), Pathfinder 1053, TM 03/13 (Manningtree & Dedham)

General description *Birdwatchers will enjoy this walk most in winter when overwintering geese and waders feed on the reservoir and estuary. But it is an enjoyable route at any season, the stretch of shore along the River Stour being particularly memorable. A pub is strategically placed for a mid-walk break. Alton Water was created in the mid-1970s to provide water for south-east Suffolk. The Tattingstone valley, an area of farmland and woodland, was dammed near Holbrook and water from the River Gipping diverted to fill it. The 3-mile- (4.75 km) long reservoir is used for various water sports and is well stocked with fish.*

The clock tower of the Royal Hospital School at Holbrook is on the right when the walk starts from the Anglian Water car park at Alton Water. Turn left to walk north-westwards along the shore. Dogs should be on leads and should never be allowed near the water. The reservoir supports many species of waterfowl, including great crested

The Tattingstone Wonder

grebes, and cormorants may be seen here in winter.

Rabbets Wood has suffered severely from storm damage though there has been extensive replanting in the vicinity. It is easy walking over the broad green sward. After Argent Manor Farm on the left the path dips into a slight valley before reaching a track going into Larch Wood. Where the track bears left away from the water take the footpath to the right to keep close to the shore. The imposing Tattingstone Place lies ahead beyond an inlet. To its left is the celebrated Tattingstone Wonder, workmen's cottages built in 1761 by the squire and disguised to look like a church. Take the path over a stile (**A**) up to the Wonder. Turn left into the lane and walk up it, past the kennels, to Bentley Lane at the top.

Turn left here and when this bends sharply to the left go ahead (**B**) down an avenue of holly trees. Predictably this track leads past Holly Farm, its fields full of fruit bushes. Beyond the pig farm turn to the right on a track heading to the right of a small wood. On its far side bear slightly to the right to continue westwards along the field edge on a narrow, well-used field path. Turn left onto the track at the end. When this meets the main street of Stutton turn right to pass the Gardeners Arms and reach the driveway to Stutton Hall with its white gateposts (**C**).

The tall chimneys of the hall can be seen at the end of the avenue of pines, but the route turns off to the right as a track crosses the drive about halfway down it (**D**). This is another pleasant field-edge track; turn left when it meets the lane going to Queech Farm.

After the farm this lane becomes a delightful sandy track which wends its way over gently folded country towards the river, which is slowly revealed. The track swings right by a large planting of conifers and descends to Stutton Mill. Here a permissive path goes off to the left at the gates of the property, following two sides of a field before turning right at a shelter belt of pines towards the river.

Turn left when the permissive path meets the shoreline right of way. Thames barges are often moored at Mistley on the southern bank of the Stour. There is a good field-edge path along the low cliffs that front this lonely shore, or you can walk on the tideline itself. Although somewhat muddy at first (this varies according to the state of the tide) the beach path becomes more sandy as you progress eastwards. The top path allows vistas inland as well as across the estuary; beyond Chestnut Spinney there are some superb parkland oak trees.

At Stutton Ness both paths swing to the north and at Graham's Wharf (**E**), where only skeletal timbers remain, they join to follow a

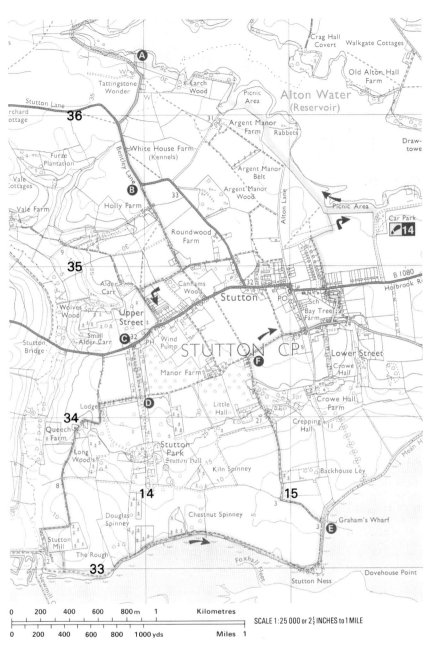

track inland which climbs up past a line of lovely old oaks. Two fine houses flank the track near the top – Little Hall on the left, Crepping Hall to the right. Turn right at a track crossroads (F), and the track soon joins with a village byway. Walk down Lower Street in the direction of the church, passing the beautiful Ancient House with its decorative plasterwork and turn left into Stutton Close just before an attractive thatched cottage. At the top of the close a footpath goes round white railings and leads to the main road.

Cross straight over the road to another field-edge footpath which passes behind houses, heading towards Alton Water. Bear right at the bottom of the field when the path meets another footpath. At the next corner turn left towards electricity poles and cross a stile which takes the path into the grounds of the reservoir. Turn right onto the path which leads back to the car park.

15 Blickling Park and the upper Bure valley

Start:	Blickling Hall, near Aylsham
Distance:	7 ½ miles (12 km). Shorter version 5 ½ miles (8·75 km)
Approximate time:	4 hours (3 hours for shorter version)
Parking:	Blickling Hall car park
Refreshments:	Pub at Wolterton, pub and seasonal tearoom at Blickling
Ordnance Survey maps:	Landrangers 133 (North East Norfolk) and 134 (Norwich & The Broads), Pathfinders 861, TG 02/12 (Aylsham & Foulsham) and 841, TG 03/13 (Holt)

General description *The richly timbered, gently rolling countryside of the upper Bure valley is a reminder of Norfolk's former beauty before the development of modern intensive farming practices. The walking is pleasant and mainly easy on sandy tracks and field paths, though some care may be needed to preserve dry feet at the river crossings where low ground surrounds the approaches to footbridges.*

The National Trust provides three car parks, all free, at Blickling, where the hall is an outstanding example of Jacobean architecture, brilliantly preserved. It was the home of Sir Thomas Boleyn, father of the future queen, though there is no evidence that Anne was born here.

Leave the main car park and turn left towards the park. Beyond the park gates bear left where the track divides, following the Weavers Way sign. The landscape of the park was carefully contrived by Humphry Repton, the lake being enlarged and woodland planted. A nineteenth-century writer described it: 'The extensive park and gardens are ornamented by a fine *lake*, extending in a crescent shape about one mile in length, and 400 yards in its greatest breadth, and skirted by verdant lawns and thickly wooded hills, rising in various forms from the pellucid water, over which the umbrageous foliage casts a shady but pleasing hue'.

Many of the scattered oaks in the park are in their prime today. Coppices of beech and pine surround old pits on the right. The track soon arrives at the Great Wood (**A**), where a diversion to the right taking a few minutes can be made to view the Earl of Buckingham's remarkable mausoleum which was built in the shape of pyramid in 1793.

Continuing on the Weavers Way, notice the Tower House in the trees on the left and leave the Great Wood where the track passes through a gate out of the park and meets a lane near a red-brick cottage. The Weavers Way bears right here, but we keep straight on along the metalled lane.

This is a delightfully leafy lane, little troubled by traffic. Just before the road junction at Itteringham Common turn to the right through a gateway (**B**). On the opposite

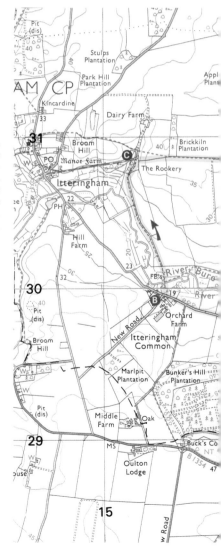

side of the road at this point there is a building with a weathercock, which looks like an old school. Cross the dyke facing you, by a metal plank bridge, and follow the path to the riverbank. In high summer the path may be partly obscured by tall foliage, and may well be boggy at any time of the year. Cross the river by the footbridge and then bear right almost immediately over another bridge. Head across the meadow ahead, bearing slightly left towards a gateway with a stile backed by two oak trees. Go through this and then follow a very pleasant path through a long meadow with the river on the left —

SCALE 1:25 000 or 2½ INCHES to 1 MILE

Spectacular autumnal colour in Blickling Park

watch for herons — and the hedge on the right. Cross a stile by the corner of a wood and follow the yellow arrow, walking along the edge of the wood.

A track comes out of the wood on the left, passing through a gate. Directly opposite this, in the hedgerow on your right, look for a stile (**C**) which takes a footpath along the right-hand edge of a field. Then cross a stile at the end of the field — now the hedge is on the left. There is a fine view to the right over the valley. Pass a footpath sign to enter a farm track and walk straight down this to pass to the left of White House Cottage. The sandy track passes through lovely countryside and the Weavers Way rejoins the route at (**D**) just before a signboard for White House Farm, Itteringham.

At this point those wishing to do only the shorter version of the walk can turn right here. The path becomes very muddy just before the footbridge over the River Bure. Cross the bridge, which is on a sharp bend of the river, and follow the path on the other side to a lane. Bear right and follow the quiet lane by the river to Blickling Mill. The lane then climbs up by the side of Great Wood to a red-brick cottage on the right which was mentioned earlier. Turn left just beyond the cottage to retrace your steps along the Weavers Way into the Great Wood, and within forty minutes you should be back at Blickling Hall.

Continue along the track until just before Fring Wood Farm where another track (**E**) leaves to the left, signposted to the Saracen's Head pub. Before it reaches Oak Cottage look to the left for a sight of Wolterton Hall, built for Horatio Walpole between 1727 and 1741 to designs by Ripley. Horatio was the cousin of Sir Robert Walpole, the famous statesman.

The track emerges at the Saracen's Head, Wolterton's unusual and very isolated pub (**F**). The landlord says that the building was put up by Walpole because he was attracted by the notion of having a Tuscan-style coaching inn on his estate. It was probably used by visiting servants as well as by ladies of Walpole's household who would watch the progress of field sports from its top windows.

Turn right at the pub to walk down the lane towards Calthorpe. At Manor Farm turn to the right down Scarrow Beck Lane and then take the first turning right to reach the group of cottages known as Lowlands.

You are now on the Weavers Way again. Turn right to follow the lane round by Fring Wood, and at its southern corner turn left along a sandy track, following a Weavers Way signpost. At the end of the track bear left onto a field-edge path with the hedge on the right. Do not take the first stile into the meadow on the right but continue to a second stile bearing a Weavers Way badge. Cross this and walk through the meadow, keeping the hedge close to the left, to reach a footbridge over the Bure — note the woodcarvings on its end rails.

After the bridge cross a long, wet meadow to low-lying woodland at the far end, where there is another footbridge and a long causeway over muddy ground. After the duck-boarding the path crosses a stile to come out onto a lane. Turn right and then immediately left (**G**) just before the cottages. Keep the hedge on the right around the field. The path soon passes a welcome seat at the entrance to Blickling Park. Follow the track back to Blickling village and the starting point.

16 Houghton, Harpley and the Peddars Way

Start:	The intersection of the Peddars Way with the Harpley to Anmer road
Distance:	7½ miles (12 km)
Approximate time:	3½ hours
Parking:	Parking on wide verge at the start
Refreshments:	Pub at Harpley
Ordnance Survey maps:	Landranger 132 (North West Norfolk) and Pathfinder 859, TF 62/72 (King's Lynn (North) & Sandringham)

General description *The return leg along the Peddars Way must be the chief glory of this walk. It is one of its finest stretches, climbing to high ground with wide views but hardly any houses in sight. For much of the time the western hedgerow survives in its wild state, and all along the route there is an abundance of blackberries and elderberries. Earlier in the walk there are pleasant interludes in woodland and along quiet country lanes.*

Refer to map overleaf.

Although the Peddars Way looks inviting at the start, leave it for later and head east on the road to Harpley, with woods on the left. Look for an opening on the left after five minutes — just beyond the tumulus on the opposite side — and follow the track straight into the woods. There is a good mixture of deciduous trees and conifers, and often deer can be seen, sometimes at quite close quarters. Carry straight on through a clearing, after which the balance between broad-leaved trees and pines shifts to the latter's advantage, and then turn to the right off the main track before this turns sharply left. Bear left when this path forks, making for the cottage dimly seen through the trees ahead. On emerging from the wood cross the field to the cottage and turn right onto the track which follows the edge of the wood. Note the magnificent beech tree on the left before the field of pigs on the other side.

At the end of the pigs' field turn left onto a driveway flanked by broad grassy verges which meets the road at West Lodge. Take a few paces to the left for a distant view of Houghton Hall, the home of the Marquess of Cholmondeley, but then return and continue south-eastwards along the road, which forms a boundary of the deer park.

This is a pleasant part of the route along a quiet, leafy lane with fine trees all around. Carry straight on at the first junction at Old Bottom and also where the road to Anmer goes off to the right. You are now on a lane even less disturbed by traffic; round bales of straw are sometimes stacked on its broad verges.

Turn left off this broad avenue onto the lane to Harpley (**A**). The lane becomes narrow and twisty just beyond the barn but soon broadens again. Note the old craters in the fields on the left, reminders of dramas of fifty years ago when crippled bombers returning to base, probably nearby Bircham, ditched their bombloads before attempting an emergency landing. The noise of traffic on the King's Lynn to Fakenham road interrupts the tranquillity. Cross straight over the main road and Back Street and turn right into Church Lane.

Look for a triangulation point on the left (**B**) just before a wood. A footpath runs down the edge of this wood, though you may prefer to visit Harpley church first. This is a few yards further along the lane and is a particularly fine building — surprisingly

Harpley church

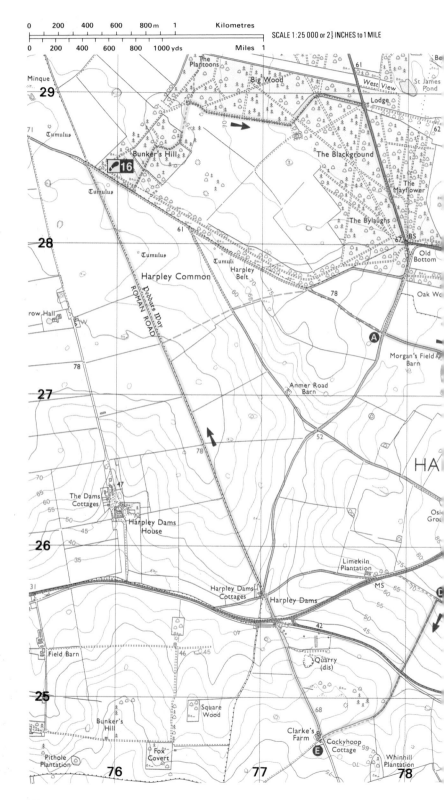

spacious and with a Saxon piscina and outstanding medieval woodwork.

The path by the wood leads onto a lane. Turn right, and then right again when this meets another lane. Just before the Rose and Crown pub, which serves bar snacks and more ambitious meals, turn into a sandy lane (**C**) on the left between wooden fences, by a footpath sign. For a short distance this becomes a refreshing green lane but then it deteriorates into a narrow path between wild hedges. It leads to a meadow with a stile over an electric fence. Cross the following field diagonally, heading for a stile near the left corner where the path joins with a bridleway.

This is a lovely ancient thoroughfare with blackberry-bearing brambles on each side. It heads back towards the main road, but before reaching it turn left (**D**) downhill on the main track. This is one of Norfolk's rare steep hills! At the bottom the track crosses a lane and the old railway. Pass through the gate which faces you − it has on it a badge saying that this is part of a Peddars Way circular walk. The final part of this leg of the walk is along the edge of a field to Clarke's Farm and Cockyhoop Cottage. Turn right onto the Peddars Way (**E**).

There are lovely views as the track dips down towards the main road. Here an incongruous note is struck by the British Pipeline Agency's gas pumping station on the right and the Paradise Dogotel on the left.

On the other side of the main road civilisation is soon left behind as the Peddars Way climbs steadily up a long sandy hill. At the top it becomes a broad grassy track. If you had to visualise ideal walking in Norfolk this would be it − an undulating way with limitless views on either side. On the left there is a rare phenomenon for this part of the world − an untamed, wholly natural hedge. Too soon Houghton Woods come into view on the right and shortly afterwards you meet the road which leads back to the starting point.

The Peddars Way

17 Five south Norfolk villages

Start:	Ashwellthorpe
Distance:	7½ miles (12 km)
Approximate time:	3½ hours
Parking:	By Ashwellthorpe church (except at times of church services). Park on right-hand side of the green as you face the church
Refreshments:	Pubs at Ashwellthorpe and Wreningham
Ordnance Survey maps:	Landranger 144 (Thetford & Breckland) and Pathfinder 923, TM 09/19 (Attleborough & Ashwellthorpe)

General description *This walk passes through five sleepy villages typical of south Norfolk. The presence of the Tacolneston TV mast close by testifies to this being comparatively high land, and the views over the village of Hapton and the valley of the River Tas seem limitless. Most of the way is on well-walked paths or byways, and there is a delightful stretch following a stream through woodland glades.*

Before starting, glance inside beautiful Ashwellthorpe church. Although small it contains several interesting features, including a famous monument to an early squire of the village, Sir Edmund de Thorpe, who was slain at a siege in Normandy and brought home for burial here. His effigy, and that of his wife, are carved from white marble, feet resting on greyhounds.

Turn left along the main road from the church. Fundenhall church can be clearly seen across the fields on the right. When the road swings to the left take the clearly marked bridleway on the right (**A**), a good field-edge path which comes to a short loke leading to a lane close to St Nicholas' Church, Fundenhall. This is a very small, remote village notable for its post office, which is in a farmhouse, and telephone exchange. The small church is kept locked since it was vandalised some years ago. Pass it to reach the main road by the hut which houses the telephone exchange.

Go straight across the main road onto a well-used field-edge path, which can be muddy at first. The view ahead, across the lovely valley of the River Tas, improves as you progress. The path crosses a disused railway line, over a bridge. Unfortunately the cutting below has been adapted as a scrapyard. This was once a sort of railway bypass, a loop line which allowed trains from places in the east, such as Beccles, to reach west Norfolk, the Midlands and the north without going through Norwich. Journey times, however, may seem excessive to us today — in 1922 it took four hours to get from Beccles to King's Lynn on this route.

The track continues eastwards to join with a lane below Hapton church. Climb up to the church, which is usually left unlocked. Peep inside to appreciate its simple beauty. Turn right at the road junction after the church and follow the lane down to the main road. Just as you reach this look for a footpath sign on the left pointing up the left side of a field. Follow this to join with the drive to the farm.

Fork left (**B**) before the farmhouse, Hapton Hall, and then bear right to pass through the farmyard and join with another drive from the hall. Where this emerges in the village of Flordon turn left along the lane. Flordon church is on the right, reached by a footpath leading uphill by new houses. Its tower fell down in the eighteenth century.

Just beyond the road junction, and before the mushroom farm, look for a footpath on

the left (**C**) leading into a low-lying meadow. The path reaches a stream on the far side of this field, and then follows its course through a long wood. This is the highlight of the walk, especially at bluebell time. The meandering course of the stream and its sparkling water beneath a canopy of foliage is a refreshing delight. Shetland ponies roam the wood, which is part of Flordon Common. At the end of this section keep to the left to reach the road over a stile made of scaffolding poles.

Turn right along the lane and then after ½ mile (0.75 km) turn left through a gateway (**D**), opposite a white gate. Walk along the grassy ridge, with the hedge on the right. Most of the old sand-pit has been infilled. A narrow path leads round its edge and descends to a bridge over the stream. Cross the field keeping to the left side of the spinney ahead.

Cross a plank bridge over a ditch and follow the field edge. The stream soon reappears on the right, and the path crosses the hedgeline to follow its course more closely. Turn right at the lane, which leads to a handful of houses at Toprow, including a post office on the left, and then cross the main road to Mill Lane on the other side.

This leads to the centre of Wreningham. A footpath to the right before the market garden leads to Wreningham church and is also the safest way to the Bird in Hand pub, a diversion of about 1 mile (1.5 km). Otherwise continue to the heart of the village, the crossroads by the school, and go straight over, following the signpost to Wymondham. The mixture of housing in Wreningham is typical of many Norfolk villages, with smartly restored old cottages standing next to modern properties built in fashionable red brick. There are still a handful of cottages which survive in more-or-less traditional form, nicely unsmartened.

After the disused railway bridge, where the road bends sharply to the right, bear left on the track to Old Rectory Farm (**E**). Walk past the farm and then a paddock on the right. Beyond the paddock the field-edge path curves to the left before turning sharply to the right. At this corner − once the site of a cottage, as fragments of china and glass in the field testify − there is a plank bridge across the ditch. Cross this and then the field ahead, walking towards a planting of saplings opposite. The young trees have been planted at the end of a farm track.

The hedge at the end of the track heads towards a wood. Follow the right-hand side of the hedge and when it ends cross the ditch on the left by another plank bridge. Continue to the edge of the wood − the right of way cuts across the corner of a field. Turn left to follow the path around the edge of the wood towards Ashwellthorpe. After a second plank bridge turn left away from the wood to follow a hedgerow to reach Ashwellthorpe Street. The White Horse pub is now close on your right; the church, the starting point of this walk, is an equal distance to the left.

SCALE 1:25 000 or 2½ INCHES to 1 MILE

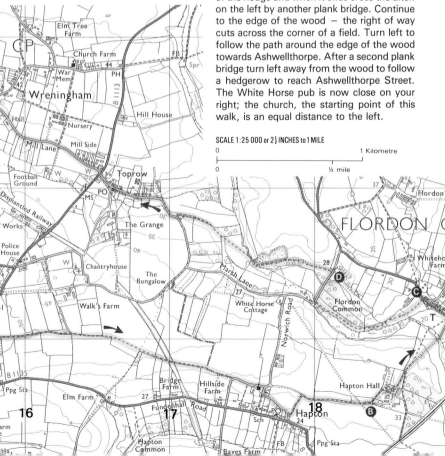

18 River Bure walk

Start:	Upton
Distance:	7 miles (11·25 km)
Approximate time:	3½ hours
Parking:	Car park at Upton Dyke
Refreshments:	Pub at Upton, just off route
Ordnance Survey maps:	Landrangers 133 (North East Norfolk) and 134 (Norwich & The Broads), Pathfinders 883, TG 21/31 (Norwich (North) & Wroxham) and 884, TG 41/51 (Caister-on-Sea & Ormesby Broad)

General description The full character of Broadland is caught on these paths. The views are limitless, often through 360 degrees, and a wide variety of habitats for birds, beasts and plants ensures constant interest for the naturalist. The return stretch by green road and through woodland is almost as enjoyable as the riverbank outward journey.

Upton Dyke has two memorials to the history of the Broads. The wherry *Maud* lies in Eastwood Whelpton's boatyard, one of two surviving craft of this type. She was built in 1900 and lay as a hulk for nearly thirty years before being rescued for restoration. Close by is Palmer's hollow post mill — the only windpump of this type remaining. It may occasionally be seen working.

Leaving these reminders of the past, walk along the left-hand side of the dyke. Most craft moored here seem to be sailing boats. It is only a short distance to the main river — the Bure, one of the main thoroughfares of the Broads which is very busy in high summer but nearly deserted in winter months. Follow the path along its banks, which even out of season is well trodden by anglers. Occasionally it leaves the riverbank to run for a time at the riverbank's base, allowing the flora here to be inspected at close quarters.

The derelict Oby Mill, built in 1753, can be seen on the opposite bank. A little way beyond this the path passes Upton Mill. The tower has been converted into a home, and today an electric pump works close by. The rusting remains of a boiler among the nettles shows that steam followed wind power for a time here; subsequently an oil engine also operated, before being superseded by electricity.

After the mill the path again descends to the foot of the bank, giving views of the grazing marshes almost at eye level. A wealth of bird life may be seen through the seasons: in winter golden plovers flock here, while redshanks and oyster-catchers, with greylag geese which graze among the cattle, are present through most of the year. The path bends westwards at Thurne Mouth (**A**), where there is a convenient seat to rest and watch the traffic on the two rivers.

The path continues along the bank of the Bure towards St Benet's Abbey, which can be seen straight ahead, though this is deceptive as the distance to be walked is greatly increased by the sinuous twists of the river. In summer there is a wonderful display of butterflies — red admirals are the most common and there are also tortoiseshells. If you are really lucky you may catch sight of the rare swallowtail.

The path winds by fine willow trees and the outer works of St Benet's may now be seen

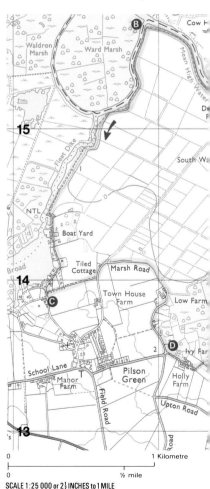

SCALE 1:25 000 or 2½ INCHES to 1 MILE

on the opposite bank, showing the extent of the large monastery which once thrived here. It was founded in 1020 on land granted by King Canute and grew to become one of the wealthiest Benedictine houses of the realm, reaching the height of its prosperity in the Middle Ages but declining before the Reformation. Thus it seems it was not worth Henry VIII's while to dissolve the abbey. The Bishop of Norwich still holds the title of Abbot of St Benet's and attends a service in the grounds each year.

Beyond St Benet's the path bears left (**B**) along the bank of Fleet Dyke, where the going is slightly rougher, although Anglian Water and the Broads Authority have been at pains to keep the path clear. Moored boats herald the approach of South Walsham, and the path leaves the bank of the cut to join Fleet Lane which runs behind moorings. At the Stores (open in summer for ice creams and drinks) there is a good view of South Walsham Broad.

After the Staithe car park at South Walsham the lane bears sharply left. At this point look for a footpath on the left (**C**) which follows the left-hand side of a field. Turn left when the path meets Marsh Road and pass Tiled Cottage before forking right to continue along the pleasant green lane waymarked with the Broads Authority's green arrow.

This leads past a large thatched barn on the right and then a lovely cottage, Marsh Lodge, on the left. Continue along the lane to a driveway on the left marked 'Private' (**D**), which is nonetheless the footpath. Pass through the farmyard of Holly Farm and at the end, with chicken houses on the right, turn to the left following a footpath sign towards woods. The path threads through the edge of the woods, a delightful part of the walk. Narrow planks aid progress over places which are boggy when the weather has been wet.

Eventually the path emerges onto the edge of a field. It then leads to the modern housing of Cargate Green. Turn left here (**E**) along the lane. Carry straight on at Marsh Road but bear left at Boat Dyke Road to reach the car park at Upton Dyke.

19 Pingoland and Thompson Water

Start: Stow Bedon on west side of the Watton to Swaffham road (A1075)

Distance: 8 miles (12·75 km)

Approximate time: 4 hours

Parking: Great Eastern Pingo Trail car park at the former station at Stow Bedon

Refreshments: Pub at Thompson

Ordnance Survey maps: Landranger 144 (Thetford & Breckland) and Pathfinder 922, TL 89/99 (Mundford & Great Hockham)

General description *The Great Eastern Pingo Trail is a new walk which takes the rambler into a unique landscape. Pingos are features of glaciation. During the Ice Age, about 20,000 years ago, water was frozen beneath the ground, forming large, lens-like blocks of ice which pushed up the soil; when they melted they left crater-like depressions scattered about the countryside which have become known to geologists as pingos. The official trail follows a shorter route which allows close examination of the pingos on its return leg from Thompson Water; much of this route, however, goes through a nature reserve where dogs are not permitted. Our route offers an alternative, both for dog owners and for those liking a longer walk, which passes one of the most picturesque pubs in Norfolk.*

The car park for the Great Eastern Pingo Trail occupies the yard of the former Stow Bedon station. The railway line, which ran from Thetford to Swaffham and was affectionately known as the 'Crab and Winkle', was closed in 1965. The 1922 edition of Bradshaw shows that five passenger trains ran in each direction daily, the 23-mile (37 km) trip taking just under an hour. Originally the land was bought from British Rail by Norfolk County Council so that a bypass might be built round Great Hockham using the trackbed of the disused railway. However, the bypass was rerouted and this section of the old railway was eventually made into a footpath (though not an official right of way – the council emphasises that those using it do so at their own risk).

From the car park head for the derelict black station house ahead, passing it on the path to its right. Local schoolchildren have incorporated a pingo into their miniature nature reserve which they created adjacent to the car park for a Duke of Edinburgh Award Scheme project. The meshed planking on the opening section of the walk will be encountered again later on. Many pingos are hidden in the vegetation of the wet woodland on each side of the path. They can be more easily recognised after the first stile.

After the second stile the line emerges from the dense woodland into more open countryside. At Crow's Farm the crossing-keeper's cottage lies derelict; on the far side its interior walls of clay lump are laid bare to the elements. After this the path heads for the forest, and the field on the left has irregular depressions which may once have been pingos, their outlines masked by ploughing.

More wetland follows as the line crosses Cranberry Rough, a basin mire which is the haunt of dragonflies, damselflies and a host of waterfowl. After a bridge across a drainage ditch – the wildlife is well seen from here – about 200 yards (183 m) of meshed planking takes the path over a particularly soggy section. Soon afterwards the line passes through a cutting, at the end of which (**A**) steps lead up the bank to take the path away from the railway and onto a lane.

Turn right here and bear right again when the lane joins with the Peddars Way (**B**). Fork right for a third time off the made-up road onto a track bearing the waymark of the Peddars Way long-distance footpath. This runs from the Suffolk border north-westwards to the coast at Holme next the Sea near Hunstanton, a distance of 45 miles (72 km) (joined with the Norfolk Coast Path it is 93 miles (149 km) long). The directness of its course shows that it was built by the Romans as a military route, probably either just before or soon after the uprising against them led by Queen Boudicca of the Iceni in AD 61.

This is a very pleasant section of the Peddars Way in spite of the Battle Area notices on the left of the track. A total of 17,500 acres of Breckland serve the interests of the military as a training ground and although the public are denied access there is a spin-off for wildlife, which seems to prefer the explosions caused by the military to the disturbances of normal human existence. Note the ancient, twisted Scots pines: they are original natives of Breckland, dating from the time when the area was a vast rabbit warren.

Soon after the track to Watering Farm on the right, Thompson Water can be glimpsed through the trees, also on the right (**C**). Well stocked with carp, the 40-acre artificial lake is a popular fishing venue. The Pingo Trail heads eastwards past its northern end. Our path continues along the Peddars Way.

A made-up track soon crosses the route (**D**), but keep on the Peddars Way to the next turning (**E**). Turn right after Shakers' Furze onto a wide drove which passes widely spaced ancient oak trees. Bear left when the earlier track joins and carry straight on to the village, forking right at the first thatched cottage and then left at another to pass houses on the left.

Go straight over the crossroads — there is a shop on the left — to reach the Chequers pub; carry straight on past it, and further on a footpath to Thompson church leaves the road on a right-hand bend. Our path lies

beyond this just before the next right-hand bend (**F**). Look for a faint path through the trees here — this is the beginning of the Drove Lane, an ancient bridleway which is in danger of becoming choked up. Hopefully the passage of more feet through its course will help to keep the nettles down.

This lovely old way emerges at another lane. Turn left to reach the main road and then turn right to walk about 200 yards (183 m) back to the car park.

SCALE 1:30 120 or about 2 INCHES to 1 MILE

20 Knettishall Heath and Thetford Forest

Start:	Knettishall Heath Country Park
Distance:	8 miles (12·75 km)
Approximate time:	3½ hours
Parking:	Knettishall Heath Country Park car park
Refreshments:	None
Ordnance Survey maps:	Landranger 144 (Thetford & Breckland) and Pathfinder 943, TL 88/98 (Thetford)

General description *The sandy, comparatively infertile area of south Norfolk and north-west Suffolk known as Breckland was almost a desert populated only by rabbits until the latter part of the last century. Then new agricultural practices began to show that the light soil could produce crops and a little later, in the 1920s, it was discovered that coniferous trees also flourished here. Today forestry still dominates, and it is difficult to find areas showing the original characteristics of the Breckland landscape. Much of this walk is through Thetford Forest, though there are substantial portions which give hints of what Breckland must once have looked like.*

Knettishall Heath Country Park is the official starting point of the Peddars Way, which ends 46 miles (74 km) to the north at Holme next the Sea. This walk is somewhat less ambitious. It begins by following a track through the picnic site between the road on the left and the Little Ouse River on the right. The track is waymarked by a blue-green flash and passes across heathland – primeval Breckland – where in summer there is a loud chorus from grasshoppers.

Soon trees appear ahead, while to the right there is an expanse of marshy riverside. The path skirts around deep pits on the right which may well have been bomb craters. It bends to the right to enter the wood, Blackwater Carr, which is mainly of mature oak and birch. At the footpath junction (**A**) turn right onto the Peddars Way, walking north. This is a lovely section, deciduous woodland alternating with clearings of grass and bracken. It leads to a footbridge over the Little Ouse, a stream which though murky seems to support an abundance of wildlife.

On the northern side of the river the path is more open, passing among pines until it reaches a narrow belt of trees with open fields on the right. In early summer this copse is ravaged by saw-fly larvae which strip the foliage and weave dense webs from the ground to branches at about head-height. The result resembles the special effects which adorn Hammer horror movies.

After passing what is probably an old parish boundary stone set in the middle of the path, the main Diss to Thetford road is crossed, and then a lesser road which goes towards Norwich. The path continues northwards. It is still the Peddars Way and heads towards the ford over the River Thet, but before this is reached, about ½ mile (0.75 km) after the road, look for a footpath sign on the right (**B**). Take this path through the forest; caravans may be seen half hidden among the trees on the left.

Turn left onto the driveway to Thorpe Woodlands camp site and then right in front of the old farmhouse, following a red-waymarked Forest Walk along a well-used track. A camping field is on the right. Fork to the right at a footpath sign, leaving the driveway to the Norfolk and Cambridgeshire Education Committee's camping sites.

This is very agreeable walking through Thetford Forest along a grassy track. When the path divides bear left to continue following the course of the river, and carry straight on when another path is offered on the right. This has the best features of a forest walk: the smell of pines and the feeling of solitude. The path bends gently to the right and a reassuring waymark appears.

After a field on the left the path meets a broad sandy track, Bridgham Lane (**C**), which strikes south-eastwards through the forest, absolutely straight. Turn right and follow this back to the road, passing by a broad grassy sward which is popular with picnickers. Look along the firebreaks as you pass them – deer are often to be seen here.

Cross the road and continue along the bridleway on the other side. After a short distance this meets with a lane heading to Riddlesworth (**D**). Turn right onto this pleasant byway which carries little traffic. It reaches the A1066 Diss to Thetford road opposite the driveway to Riddlesworth Hall School, where Princess Diana was a pupil.

Cross the road and walk down the drive, forking left to pass the church. About 100 yards (91 m) past the church the right of way has been diverted (**E**): turn right into what seems to have been a walled garden. The path twists its way through dense undergrowth to emerge close to the ha-ha below the lawn on the south side of the hall. Pass below the ha-ha and skirt a wood to join an attractive descending track with fields on either side. After the gate-lodge turn left along the lane which soon leads back to the Knettishall Heath starting point.

21 An Orwell walk from Pin Mill

Start:	Pin Mill
Distance:	8½ miles (13·5 km). Shorter version 5 miles (8 km)
Approximate time:	4 hours (2½ hours for shorter version)
Parking:	Car park at Pin Mill
Refreshments:	Pubs at Pin Mill, Chelmondiston, and Freston
Ordnance Survey maps:	Landranger 169 (Ipswich & The Naze) and Pathfinders 1053, TM 03/13 (Manningtree & Dedham) and 1054, TM 23/33 (Felixstowe & Harwich)

General description *Pin Mill is a favourite Suffolk beauty spot and here the path above the shore of the Orwell can get busy. Elsewhere, however, the route is quiet and there is much lovely countryside to enjoy. Part of the return leg from Freston is on paths across a succession of fields which, if planted with crops, may be difficult going.*

Leave the car park at Pin Mill and turn left towards the river and the Butt and Oyster, perhaps Suffolk's most famous inn. Enjoy the view from the waterside: there are usually some Thames barges moored here, and on summer weekends the Orwell seems the Hyde Park Corner for boating people. Turn left and cross Pin Mill Common, which is partly used as a dinghy park. At the junction of footpath and bridleway turn away from the river on the bridleway and at the next fork (**A**) leave it to carry straight on along a footpath which follows the edge of a field with the river close on the right.

The path runs along the edge of the next field in the same way before crossing the third field to a massive oak tree. Woolverstone Hall can be seen on the left; it was built in 1776 by William Berners, 'proprietor of the stately street in London called after his name'. This heralds a lovely interlude where the path threads through a wood of more fine trees to emerge by the river again to pass in front of the imposing clubhouse of the Royal Harwich Yacht Club.

Beyond this turn left (**B**) onto the concrete driveway, a right of way is signposted to Woolverstone church, and climb up the drive until, just past the entrance to the Chandlery, a footpath goes into the woods on the left. This leads onto a broad grassy drive and then bears left, away from caravans, into the trees. It comes out onto a large meadow, with Woolverstone church standing on its

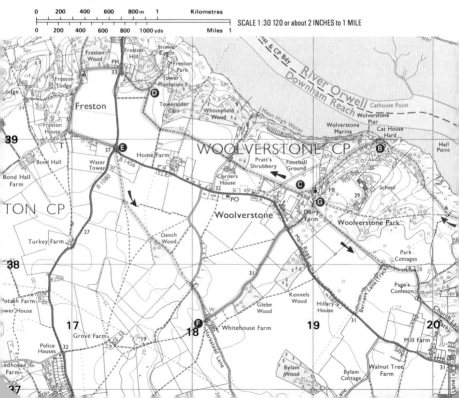

SCALE 1:30 120 or about 2 INCHES to 1 MILE

left, eastern edge. This, like the church at Freston, is often kept locked.

Those wishing to do only the shorter version of the walk can continue alongside the churchyard to its south side, cross a drive and rejoin the main route at (G).

Make for the green thatched cottage to the right of the church tower. Join the track (**C**) which runs past the cottage and follow it to the end of the meadow, where it crosses the driveway from the marina. After crossing the next lane the right of way reverts to being a footpath, following the right-hand edge of a field. At the end of this it joins a made-up drive; keep straight on along this with Freston church ahead and Freston Tower to the right. Do not take the path offered to the left which heads towards the church but continue to the next footpath junction by woods which were devastated by the hurricane of 1987. Here (**D**) there is a choice. You can continue along the track for about ½ mile (0.75 km) to visit Freston Tower retracing your steps to this point afterwards. (The tower dates from the sixteenth century and local legend has it that Lord Freston had it built for his daughter who is supposed to have been educated there, each of the six floors being used to teach her different subjects through the week — from charity on the lowest to astronomy on the roof.) But if you have seen the tower already or are suffering from terrible thirst bear left along the edge of the wood to reach the Boot, Freston's excellent pub.

To avoid walking along the main road take the lane to the left of the pub to Freston church. Walk through the churchyard and turn left to rejoin the lane on the other side, following this to Well Cottage, where you turn left again, passing the ex-school, the village hall, and the Old Rectory before crossing the Holbrook road to a field opening opposite (**E**). Walk across this field, trying to

keep to the line shown on the map, with the water tower on your right; you should reach the hedgerow about 50 yards (46 m) from the tower. Now head for a distinctive post by the power lines on the other side of the next field, and cross the following one diagonally to the corner of Dench Wood.

Keep the wood on the right to the end of the field, and then cross straight over the next one, heading for a red-brick cottage where you reach the road. Keep straight on along this to Whitehouse Farm (**F**). Turn left and walk to the end of the lane.

Cross the road to the drive to Woolverstone School and walk along it to a stile and footpath sign (**G**). Take the right-hand footpath towards Chelmondiston, bearing to the right away from the Pin Mill path to a stile by a metal fence. Climb this stile and follow the path, with the fence on the right. There is a nursery of young trees on the other side. Eventually the path joins with a bridleway at Berners Lane. The track dips down suddenly beyond Park Cottages; keep right here to pass the low ground of Page's Common, which is overlooked by weatherboarded cottages. As the track climbs turn left onto a narrow bridleway, Church Lane, which gives a lovely view of the river and Pin Mill before passing bungalows and entering Chelmondiston. Cross a road called Woodlands to reach the church, and take the lane past it on the left, Hollow Lane, to the road which leads to Pin Mill. (You could shorten the walk here should you feel tired though this would be a shame as some of the best scenery soon follows).

Cross the road to the bridleway opposite (**H**) and pass through the farmyard towards Clamp House. This is a lovely farm track, even though it has deep puddles after wet weather. The river is soon glimpsed ahead. There is a glorious scene as the track begins its descent down to Clamp House — rich woodland all about and a small lake as a foreground to the Orwell (see front cover).

Take the stile to the left at Clamp House (**J**), passing a black shed to reach it. This leads into a wood — the National Trust's Pin Mill Cliff Plantation. Although it was obviously badly damaged by the hurricane, enough trees survive to make walking a pleasure, and much replanting has been undertaken. There are delightful glimpses of the Orwell through gaps in the trees. The undulating path becomes a part of a 1-mile (1.5 km) circular route waymarked from Pin Mill. Bear off the main path towards the river following one of its yellow arrows. Now the footpath follows the shore closely, allowing fascinating glimpses of the various craft used as residences. Take the steps on the left before the Butt and Oyster pub to reach the road just above the car park.

22 'Ted Ellis Country'

Start:	Bramerton
Distance:	8 miles (12·75 km)
Approximate time:	4 hours
Parking:	Off the road parking at Bramerton Common
Refreshments:	Pubs at Bramerton Wood's End, Surlingham and Rockland St Mary
Ordnance Survey maps:	Landranger 134 (Norwich & The Broads) and Pathfinder 903, TG 20/30 (Norwich (South))

General description *Ted Ellis was a much loved and respected Norfolk naturalist who died in 1986. He lived in an idyllic marshland cottage at Wheatfen Broad, Surlingham, where there is one of the few remaining stretches of unspoilt Broadland fen and an important area of ancient woodland. David Bellamy has said of Wheatfen 'It is probably the best bit of fenland we have because we know so much about it. That is purely because one man gave his life to trying to understand it — Ted Ellis.' Apart from this the walk follows an interesting riverbank backed by marshes protected by the RSPB, and has typical stretches of quiet Norfolk lanes and field paths which pass several medieval churches.*

The River Yare at Bramerton

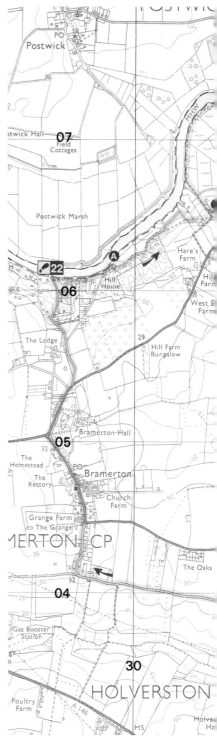

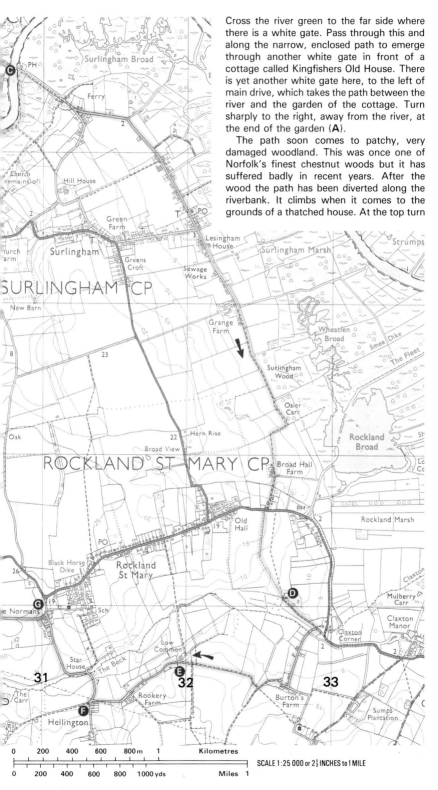

Cross the river green to the far side where there is a white gate. Pass through this and along the narrow, enclosed path to emerge through another white gate in front of a cottage called Kingfishers Old House. There is yet another white gate here, to the left of main drive, which takes the path between the river and the garden of the cottage. Turn sharply to the right, away from the river, at the end of the garden (**A**).

The path soon comes to patchy, very damaged woodland. This was once one of Norfolk's finest chestnut woods but it has suffered badly in recent years. After the wood the path has been diverted along the riverbank. It climbs when it comes to the grounds of a thatched house. At the top turn

SCALE 1:25 000 or 2½ INCHES to 1 MILE

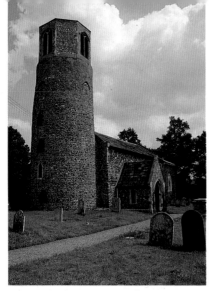

Surlingham's round-towered church

right onto the drive coming from this house and then left to enter another fenced-off path which leads to Surlingham church. This, with its round tower, is the oldest of Surlingham's two churches. The ruins of the later church lie about ½ mile (0.75 km) to the north-east, Ted Ellis is buried in its churchyard.

From the church (**B**) take the RSPB path down to the river. Keep dogs under strict control as this is part of the RSPB's Church Marsh Reserve. The last few yards to the river follow a lovely old dyke where you may be lucky enough to see kingfishers and crested grebes. This was a section of the River Yare much painted by artists of the Norwich School. About ½ mile (0.75 km) along the riverbank you reach the RSPB hide dedicated to Ted Ellis, which gives excellent views across the marshes with their abundance of birdlife. A little further on there is another hide, the Whaley hide. After another footpath leaves on the right, at the end of the RSPB reserve, the path along the riverbank becomes less well maintained. Nevertheless progress to the Surlingham Ferry House pub is not difficult. Note the painting of the old ferry, which was abandoned in 1946, on the outside of the inn.

Turn away from the river here (**C**) along the pub driveway which passes through pleasant woodland. Bear to the left where the road forks. This lane runs straight for some way through the outskirts of Surlingham village. A road on the left leads to another riverside pub, Coldham Hall. Keep straight on at the end of The Street into The Covey. The made-up road ends at Grange Farm, but the route continues along the trackway leading to the Ted Ellis Nature Reserve. Anyone interested in natural history will enjoy a detour from footpaths here. An exhibition illustrates the

aims of the trust which looks after the reserve and there are paths through the fen and wood. There is no charge to visitors though they are requested to make a voluntary contribution to upkeep. It is a fitting memorial to a great naturalist.

Beyond the reserve keep on to the end of the track and then continue along a field edge with the wood on the left. At the end of the field turn right for 200 yards (183 m), with the hedge on the left, and then turn left, towards Broad Hall Farm, when a track is seen between crops. From this track there is a view to Rockland Broad; the track passes by the farmyard to reach a road. Should you require refreshment at this point turn left here for the New Inn at Rockland St Mary (about 300 yards (274 m)). Otherwise take the track opposite; this is allowed by the landowner since the right of way crosses a very large field on the left.

This is a lovely path descending gently through fields. Follow the right-hand side of the conifer plantation and then bear left towards a house in a deciduous wood (**D**). Look for a finger-post by a lone ash tree in the meadow which points to an opening into the grounds of the house. You will emerge on the driveway to this house, Lamb Court. Turn right at the road and then right again after 500 yards (457 m) onto the track just to the right of Burton's Farm.

At the second spinney bear right at the footpath sign. The path follows the right-hand side of the hedge up a long field, then descends to a clump of oaks and blackthorn. Now the path is more clearly defined, with a hedge on the right, and continues down towards red-roofed buildings, finally emerging on the lane at Low Common (**E**). Follow the quiet byway past Rookery Farm, on the left, and then turn right at Hellington (**F**) towards Rockland St Mary. The lane crosses the stream known as the Beck and then climbs to The Normans, the big farm at the top of the hill. Rockland church can be seen on the right among the trees. Like that at Hellington, it is a lovely church to visit, worth the short detour.

Turn left at the pond at The Normans (**G**) onto an ancient track once known as St Edmund's Lane; possibly it went to the Roman town at Caistor St Edmund. This is a lovely byway, little used by traffic, which follows a ridge for about a mile (1.5 km). You really feel on top of the world here.

Turn right at the road junction, into Bramerton, and then bear left into The Street, passing the pond and church. Turn right at Surlingham Road and then left down Mill Hill (not Easthill Lane, the previous turning offered on the left), descending a steep hill down to the river at Bramerton Common, the starting point.

23 Nelson's boyhood home and Holkham Park

Start:	Burnham Overy Staithe
Distance:	9 miles (14·5 km)
Approximate time:	5 hours
Parking:	Burnham Overy Staithe (If an exceptionally high tide is due or there are no spaces here, park cars on Lady Ann's road at Holkham and start the walk from there.)
Refreshments:	Pubs at Burnham Overy Staithe, Burnham Thorpe and Holkham, café at Holkham
Ordnance Survey maps:	Landranger 132 (North West Norfolk) and Pathfinder 819, TF 84/94 (Wells-next-the-Sea & Burnham Market)

General description This part of north Norfolk is popular with young and old alike, and this walk illustrates why. At first the route climbs up from the creeks and salt marshes of Burnham Overy through agricultural land to Burnham Thorpe, where Nelson grew up. It then strikes eastwards to Holkham Park and follows the drive past the lake and hall to the village. From here it crosses the coast road to Lady Ann's Road to reach the sea. The return is made along the fascinating shoreline – an outstandingly beautiful portion of Norfolk's coast. Note that both Lady Ann's Road and the way through the park are private roads, which are open to the public at most times by courtesy of Viscount Coke. Dogs must be on leads.

Refer to map overleaf.

Take the lane by the side of the Hero pub at Burnham Overy Staithe (Gong Lane) past the post office, which is housed in a cottage on the right. After a short distance this byway becomes a sandy track as the last houses and bungalows are left behind. There are wide views across farming land from the top of this hill. The track descends towards Burnham Overy Town; go straight on across a footpath crossroads. Turn right onto the road at the end of the track, and then left after the houses onto a field path. This leads to an old railway embankment (**A**); turn left along this, and after 150 yards (137 m) look for a well-concealed signpost on the right by a stile.

Climb the stile and cross a large meadow, heading for the left-hand corner on the far side, passing a pond on the right. The path crosses a stile in front of Burnham Thorpe church (**B**), where Nelson's father was once vicar. Tattered naval flags adorn the interior of the church and there are many mementoes of the great admiral.

Follow the track round the north and west sides of the church. This leads to the road into Burnham Thorpe village. Turn left along it to pass the pub, predictably named the Lord Nelson. Turn left again to walk past the end of the playing-field and go straight over the crossroads (the village hall is on the left: the Nelson Memorial Hall), climbing a hill which is steep for Norfolk. Turn left at the top and then after 200 yards (183 m) turn right onto a broad sandy track which heads due east between fine tall hedges.

The track leads across a road towards the dense woodland of the Holkham estate. This is invigorating walking across an open landscape with views of the sea. When the track, which is by now grassy, meets the demesne wall (**C**) turn left onto the Roman road. This follows the wall beneath overhanging beech and ilex trees (the latter are said to have sprung from seeds mixed with the leaves used for packing Lord Leicester's statuary when it was dispatched from Italy 250 years ago).

At West Lodge (**D**) turn right into Holkham Park. Dogs must be on leads through the park, and do not leave the made-up drive. The small gate on the left gives access if the main one is closed. Fields lie on each side of the drive. The tower of Holkham church can just be seen amongst the trees to the left, and to the right of this is the great monument to Thomas Coke, 1st Earl of Leicester of the second creation, who was best known as 'Coke of Norfolk' because of the brilliant reforms he introduced in agriculture at the beginning of the nineteenth century. There is a long straight after Deep Clump; the garden centre is on the left. The south front of Holkham Hall slowly appears ahead and there is an even better view once over the cattle-grid into the deer park. Note the conical ice house on the right. The hall is open daily (except Fridays and Saturdays) from the end of May to the end of September from 1.30 until 5 pm. Built in Palladian style, to the designs of William Kent who also planned the park, it was started in 1734 and took thirty years to complete.

The drive skirts the lake and then passes in front of the courtyard of the hall. The stables can be seen a little further on. Fork left at the next cattle grid, leave the park through the

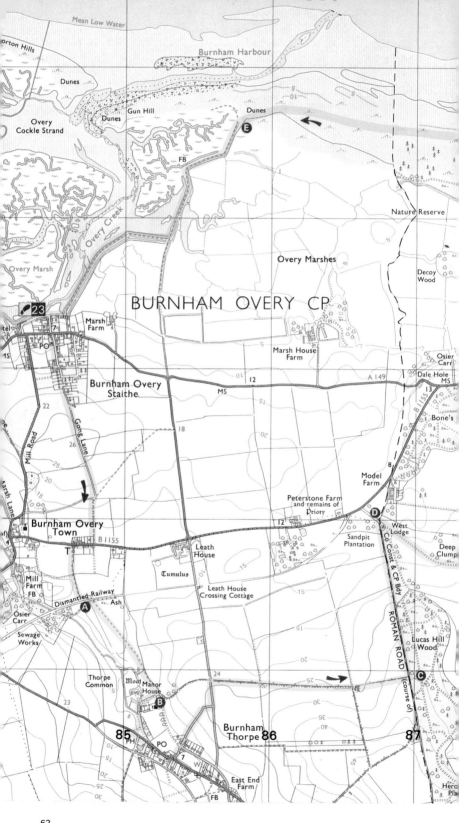

SCALE 1:25 000 or 2½ INCHES to 1 MILE

gates and go down the road lined with a fine assortment of estate houses. The Victoria Hotel is on the main road at the end.

Go straight across the main road onto Lady Ann's Road, which leads to the sea. At the end of Lady Ann's Road there is a choice of routes. Inviting paths wind westwards through the pinewood and these may be used; alternatively make for the beach and then head west. Either way shows Norfolk's coastal scenery at its best. When the pines end it is probably best to walk along the beach, although on a breezy day it may be more comfortable to continue in the shelter of the dunes. If you are on the seaward side, look for posts at the foot of the dunes which protect the nests of a colony of little terns. At the far end of the posts (E) there is a slatted path which leads to the footpath on the top of the sea defences. This follows the twists of Overy Creek back to the village and starting point.

24 Berney Arms and Breydon Water

Start:	Halvergate (from A47 Acle to Great Yarmouth road turn right to Halvergate at Stracey Arms pub and at end of road, where it turns sharply to right, take byway on left, Stone Road)
Distance:	9 miles (14·5 km)
Approximate time:	4 hours
Parking:	Off the road at Stone Road, Halvergate
Refreshments:	Pubs at Halvergate and (in holiday season) Berney Arms
Ordnance Survey maps:	Landranger 134 (Norwich & The Broads) and Pathfinder 904, TG 40/50 (Great Yarmouth & Reedham)

General description *Halvergate is one of the more remote Broadland villages, situated on the lonely marshes between Acle and Reedham. The route uses marshland tracks and paths to reach the riverbank at Berney Arms, where the sails of the tall windpump turn gently to provide a distinctive landmark. This is part of the final leg of the Weavers*

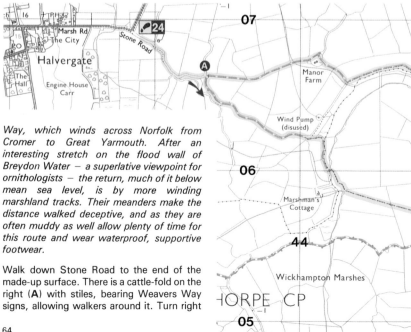

Way, which winds across Norfolk from Cromer to Great Yarmouth. After an interesting stretch on the flood wall of Breydon Water – a superlative viewpoint for ornithologists – the return, much of it below mean sea level, is by more winding marshland tracks. Their meanders make the distance walked deceptive, and as they are often muddy as well allow plenty of time for this route and wear waterproof, supportive footwear.

Walk down Stone Road to the end of the made-up surface. There is a cattle-fold on the right (**A**) with stiles, bearing Weavers Way signs, allowing walkers around it. Turn right

off Stone Road here to reach a winding, grassy track which, most of the time, heads towards the Berney Arms windpump in the far distance, its sails turning if there is a fair wind. It is flanked by two closer windpumps, both without sails. When the track is opposite the mill on the left – which still has a fantail – it bears right towards the pink-washed Marshman's Cottage.

Cross the meadow to a gate, two stiles and a bridge which takes the path across a dyke. Follow a bank on the left in the easterly direction shown by the waymark to reach another gateway (cattle often make these gateways very muddy). From here the path strikes across a broad meadow towards a new footbridge, and the Berney Arms windpump can be seen beyond it. After traversing another large meadow it reaches the track from Wickhampton (**B**); walk 20 yards (18 m) along this and then look for a footbridge across the ditch on the right. This is good smooth walking towards the mill on rich pasture. After a gate make for a bridge in the distance which looks at first like another gate. Turn left onto the right bank of the dyke. After the next gate bear left almost immediately so that you are now on the left bank of the dyke, heading towards the railway crossing – this is Berney Arms Station, just a short platform.

The RSPB Berney Marshes Reserve begins on the other side of the railway; leaflets are available from a box by the crossing. The reserve covers 1300 acres of grazing marsh and estuary, and the most important project has been to restore 366 acres into the flooded marshland habitat which existed here before modern drainage techniques allowed the cultivation of the marshes for arable crops. These acres can now be flooded in the winter to provide food for geese and waders. In spring the meadows are used as nesting sites by a wide variety of species.

The path leads directly to the windpump, which is open to visitors in the summer. Built in 1865, many consider it to be the finest of the Broadland drainage windpumps.

Turn left here (**C**) along the riverbank and pass, or pause at, the Berney Arms pub. Originally a wherryman's pub, in summer it is hectic with holidaymakers who moor here as it is the first safe place to tie up a boat before or after crossing Breydon Water.

The riverbank path passes the meeting point of the rivers Waveney and Yare and then runs along the top of the flood-wall of Breydon Water. This is a magnificent viewpoint, with Great Yarmouth clearly seen ahead, but it can be chilly up here, even in summer. An alternative path runs below it.

The route leaves Breydon Water when the railway line comes close to the flood wall at Breydon pump (**D**), a modern machine, housed in a green shed, which replaced the old Lockgate windpump whose ruins stand a little further on.

Cross the railway and take the twisting concrete track away from Breydon Water. The only landmark here is an abandoned combine, significant in that it shows the unfortunate trend, now thankfully ended, of converting these grazing marshes into arable fields. If this had continued it would have meant the end of a habitat uniquely valuable to a wide variety of birdlife. Close to this there is a Weavers Way signpost on the left (**E**). At first it seems as though this path will lead back to Berney Arms, but it soon turns westwards to wind past Marsh Cottages, on the left, and the thatched Marsh Farm, on the right. It subsequently passes two disused windpumps, the first with a fantail.

Opposite the second windpump, which is set back a short distance on the right, the track swings to the left. There are scant remains in the grass here of the building marked on the map (**F**). In winter well over 100 swans may be seen grazing the marsh on the left.

As the track gets nearer civilisation it deteriorates, cattle making it very muddy at times. Progress is also slow because of its meandering course. After Manor Farm the going improves — the track is made-up and the cattle-fold and Stone Road where the route started are soon reached.

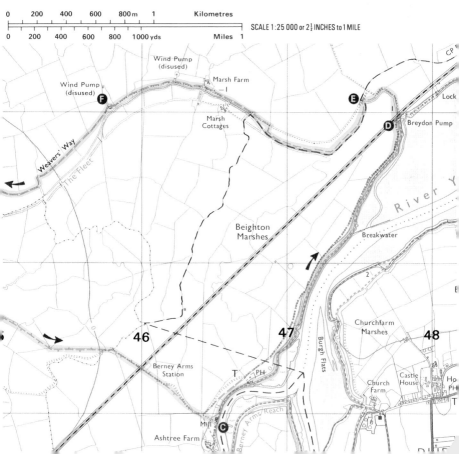

25 Framlingham and Earl Soham

Start:	Framlingham
Distance:	9½ miles (15·25 km). Shorter version 5 miles (8 km)
Approximate time:	4½ hours (2½ hours for shorter version)
Parking:	Framlingham − car park just off Well Close Square on road going round western side of the Mere
Refreshments:	Pubs and restaurants at Framlingham, pubs at Saxtead Green and Earl Soham
Ordnance Survey maps:	Landranger 156 (Saxmundham & Aldeburgh) and Pathfinder 986, TM 26/36 (Framlingham & Saxmundham)

General description *Both versions of this walk use paths which generally follow the edges of enormous fields as well as some of the ancient green tracks which are a feature of this part of east Suffolk. The opportunity should be taken of visiting the church as well as the castle at Framlingham: both buildings are of exceptional interest. The shorter walk passes very close to Saxtead Mill, the archetypal Suffolk post-mill, which is open to the public.*

The seventeenth-century diarist John Evelyn noted that Framlingham was famous for producing the tallest oak trees in Suffolk, and perhaps in the world. They were used for building the keels of the great capital ships of the navy and the tree used for the *Royal Sovereign* gave four beams, each 44 feet (13 m) long. The oaks grew in the vast deer park which once surrounded Framlingham Castle. This looks a formidable stronghold from the Mere, its long curtain-wall with twelve towers enclosing an area of well over

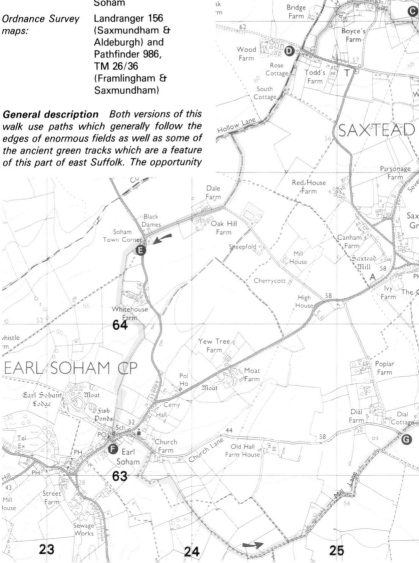

an acre. Unfortunately there is little to see of the original castle inside the great walls, all the interior apartments having been stripped out in 1650 in order to provide material for building the almshouses and workhouse sited within the walls of the castle at the bequest of the last private owner, Sir Robert Hitcham.

There was a castle at Framlingham in Saxon times which was rebuilt by the Bigods after the Conquest. The stronghold that we see today dates from about 1200 and shows that the Crusaders had learned that a keep was no longer a prime necessity for a castle, which could be better defended by a strong curtain-wall with towers. The stone for the castle came from Barnack in Northamptonshire, and was brought to the site by boats sailing up the River Ore, where there is barely enough water to float a child's boat today.

Turn right out of the car park onto the road which goes round the western side of the Mere, and turn right off this road to take a footpath which skirts the shore of the lake, providing a lovely foreground to the castle walls beyond. Rejoin the road before the playing-field and at the end of the playing-field on the left (after the drive which leads through it) turn left (**A**) on a footpath which crosses a ditch by an iron-grid bridge to enter a large meadow. Bear slightly right and walk uphill to pass to the left of a barn through a gateway bearing a red circular walk badge. To the right is the depot of a plant-hire company. In the next field walk away from its yard, heading for the top right-hand corner.

Cross a stile here and carry straight on, following the ditch which is on the right to reach Durrant's Bridge. Go straight over the Dennington road here and continue following the path – the sword with BW on the signpost is the logo for the Bigod Way – along field edges and by a new plantation of conifers. The accompanying ditch to the right is the majestic River Ore. Continue

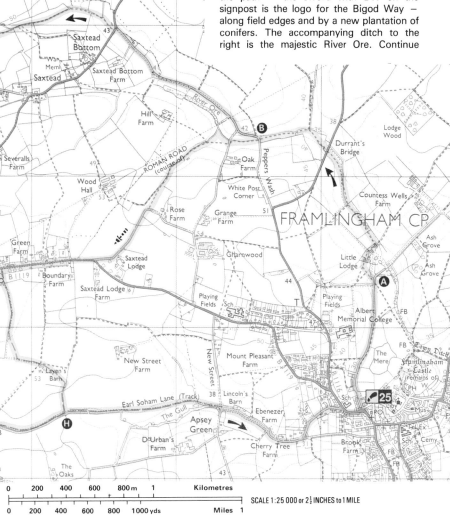

along the path to the lane known as Peppers Wash (**B**).

At this point, those wishing to do only the shorter version of the walk can cross Peppers Wash to continue on the field path, still following the circular walk sign, and continue across the next road as well. The ditch on the right is no longer the River Ore after the path makes a sharp left turn. When it meets the lane to Rose Farm keep straight on along the lane, heading for the main road.

When the lane joins the B1119 follow the road into Saxtead Green (after Boundary Farm the green is wide enough to walk on a footpath away from the busy road!). Ignore the first footpath sign on the left and continue to the bridleway on the same side, opposite the telephone-box. (If you wish to visit the pub or Saxtead Mill keep on for a little way further and return to this point.)

Fork left on the bridleway soon after the start to follow the farm track across the prairie-like fields. Turn left again, keeping on the main track when the bridleway divides. At the site of the former Layen's Barn continue to follow the bridleway round the field edge to reach the track known as Earl Soham Lane, which is the final leg of the longer route. Turn left here to return to Framlingham.

Turn right onto Peppers Wash, and ignore the left turn after 200 yards (183 m) to reach the Dennington road at Saxtead Bottom. Turn slightly left to cross the road to the footpath by the wooden railings. A pleasant walk along the field edge follows on a generous headland. Saxtead church is in the clump of trees to the left. A footpath sign points across the field towards isolated trees, showing where a hedge once grew. The route continues to follow the field edge. Keep the hedge on the right as the path skirts round two small fields. When confronted by a rickety gate (**C**) climb this carefully to reach a narrow meadow. Walk through this and the following L-shaped meadow to reach the road, past a lovely yellow-painted house. Turn right and follow the lane round to a road. Turn right here, and at the crossroads turn left (**D**) down Hollow Lane.

After South Cottage this becomes a field track which at first crosses flat and hedgeless countryside. It soon improves and looks quite inviting ahead when a large bridleway sign points off to the left towards Dale Farm. Take this route to reach the road, and pass the lovely farm with its duckpond. Follow the road the short distance to Soham Town Corner (**E**). Go straight across here, following a footpath sign which points along the field edge to the right of a newish bungalow. Carry straight on at the footpath junction to follow the shallow valley with Whitehouse Farm on the left. Keep the hedge and ditch to

Framlingham Castle

the left until the way seems blocked ahead. Turn left over a footbridge so that the ditch is now on the right. Earl Soham church tower can now be seen to the left. The path leads into a playing-field with the village school on the far side. Keep to the right, passing behind the school, to cross a bridge and reach the main road (**F**). The pub is a very short distance to the right, though the way back to Framlingham lies to the left.

At the church turn to the right up Church Lane and before this reaches Church Farm turn right to follow a footpath sign which is well concealed in the hedge. Cross the plank bridge and take the path which follows field edges towards the left side of a small wood. Cross the ditch before the wood and at the end of it follow the track, with the hedge first to the right and then to the left. This is a well-used path, by horse-riders as well as walkers. Where the footpath meets a bridleway keep straight on along the path towards a small wood, now with the hedge to the left. Although a bit churned up by horses, Mill Lane is a delightful track, winding through fields screened by hedges on both sides.

The route joins with a short stretch of made-up road which it leaves when the road bends sharply to the left before Dial Cottage (**G**). This is Earl Soham Lane. Saxtead Mill can be glimpsed on the left at the end of a belt of trees just after the track twists to the left-hand side of the hedge.

Pass a junction with a footpath and then cross a bridge with iron guardrails over a ditch. The shorter version of the walk, from Layen's Barn, joins at the next junction (**H**). Keep straight on here through a short stretch of semi-sunken lane. The final part of this walk is similar to Mill Lane earlier – passing between tall hedges as it drops down to the deep ditch strangely known as the Gull.

At the lane turn right over the bridge and then immediately left. After Ebenezer Farm, at the 30 mph sign, turn left down another lane to reach the main road into Framlingham. Turn right here, opposite the primary school, to reach Well Close Square. The car park and starting point are to the left.

26 Marriott's Way and Drayton Drewray

Start:	Drayton, 2 miles (3·25 km) west of Norwich
Distance:	10 miles (16 km)
Approximate time:	4 hours
Parking:	Marriott's Way car park at Costessey Lane, Drayton
Refreshments:	Pubs at Drayton and Felthorpe
Ordnance Survey maps:	Landranger 133 (North East Norfolk) and Pathfinder 882, TG 01/11 (Lenwade)

General description *The outward section of the walk uses a part of Marriott's Way, a 7-mile (11.25 km) walk along the track of a disused railway between Hellesdon on the outskirts of Norwich and Attlebridge on the upper reaches of the River Wensum. William Marriott was chief engineer and general manager of the Midland & Great Northern Railway Company (M&GN), which once owned this track. A formidable but well-loved figure, he ran the railway for 41 years. The homeward section runs across farmland and through two patches of woodland, and is especially beautiful in spring.*

Refer to map overleaf.

Leave the car park and turn right onto Costessey Lane to the main road which runs through Drayton. Turn left and then immediately left again onto the lane to Taverham. After The Crescent look for the Marriott's Way entrance (**A**), on the right and descend into a deep cutting. This was cut through chalk, and thirteen skeletons were discovered during its excavation. It has been suggested that they were victims of the Black Death hastily buried in a plague pit.

Cross the main road and enter another cutting, which in spring is ablaze with broom. There are glimpses of extensive housing developments through the trees, but soon these are left behind and the railway track heads into open countryside. The gradient up to the bridge over Breck Farm Lane must have meant hard shovelling for the locomotives' firemen in bygone days, though walkers will hardly notice the hill. Keep to the course of the old railway line at Freeland Corner.

The M&GN was always a little sister to the major railway company of East Anglia, the Great Eastern. It provided an alternative link between Norwich and the Midlands and north, running into the now vanished City station in Norwich. Passing through underpopulated countryside with few towns of any size it was never very profitable and was closed to passengers in 1959. It must have been near here that one of the most celebrated incidents in the building of the railway occurred. Two engineers' trains met head-on, and neither driver being prepared to back off, they fought out the right of way with bare fists, Little Billy Walker being the victorious driver.

After Freeland Corner the road runs close to the line, as it does through Mileplain Plantation. The track was laid very straight through the wood here, and the permanent way gang must have had to work hard to keep undergrowth cut back.

A little way beyond the bridge Marriott's Way emerges into open country again. The Wensum valley lies to the left, with Ringland Hills beyond. Just beyond a modern house with a radio mast turn right on steps down the embankment to reach a field-edge path heading north-east (**B**).

Go straight across the main road onto a track which soon descends into Upgate (**C**). Cross the road to the village noticeboard and continue along a track towards a converted barn with a dovecot. After 50 yards (46 m), where the track bends left, keep straight on, following a footpath over the common. There is a pond on the right and then a newly converted house with stables. Follow the riders' track from this — it is marked with posts with horseshoes fixed to them — through lovely woodland. There is soon a large field on the right; follow as closely as possible to the fence by this until you reach a stile. Climb this and walk across the field towards farm buildings on the far side — the path is likely to be well defined at most times of the year. Most of the farm buildings are derelict chicken sheds. Walk past these and just before the road take a track on the left

Marriott's Way

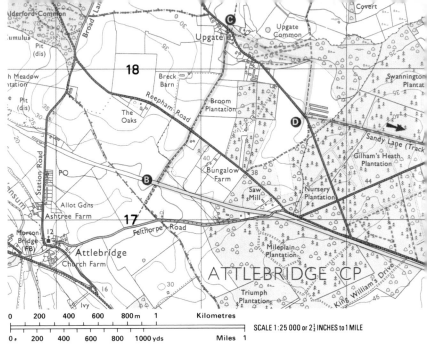

SCALE 1:25 000 or 2½ INCHES to 1 MILE

which runs parallel to the concrete foundations of a vanished shed. This (**D**) is the western end of Sandy Lane which, muddy at first in spite of its name, leads through more woodland.

When Sandy Lane meets the road to Felthorpe turn left and then immediately right onto another woodland path. Keep straight on at a footpath junction to leave the woods past a 'No Horses' sign. An ancient path enclosed with holly trees leads to the Taverham Road. Turn left into Felthorpe and follow the lane round two bends and then turn right onto Church Lane.

This leads to St Michael's Church, which dates from 1694 although it looks much older. Turn left to visit it, or right to continue the walk down Brand's Lane. This was once a popular thoroughfare with smugglers who probably made up the story of it being haunted by a headless man running beside a cart. Mary Sewell, mother of Anna, the author of *Black Beauty*, recounted this story in her memoirs. She lived in Felthorpe in the nineteenth century.

Turn left (**E**) off the lane towards a wood, over new stiles on the left side of a field shortly before a modern house. Once in the wood bear right onto the main path. Where this divides fork right and then turn left and almost immediately right at the next junction, among rhododendrons. This is Drayton Drewray, part of Felthorpe Woods, an extensive area of woodland. It was common land until its enclosure in 1813, the late date of this giving a clue to its lack of value because of its infertility. Turn left and immediately right again at the next junction,

following the waymark, to leave the wood past a concrete footpath sign.

The right of way now follows a field-edge track towards Bell Farm. Turn right (**F**) before the farm and its attractive pond onto another farm track (the farmer prefers walkers to take this route rather than following the right of way through the farmyard).

Cross straight over the main road at the end of this farm track onto a lane leading past two new schools, and the original village school converted into a residence, into Drayton village. Bear right at the junction to pass the half-thatched church which dates from the thirteenth century and was drastically restored in the nineteenth. Go straight across the main road to reach Costessey Lane, which is to the left of the garage.

The parish church at Drayton

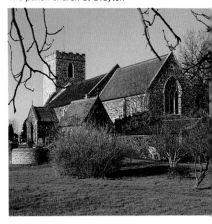

70

27 Sheringham Park and Pretty Corner

Start:	Sheringham Park (entrance is at junction of A148 and B1157, Upper Sheringham)
Distance:	11½ miles (18·5 km)
Approximate time:	5 hours
Parking:	National Trust car park, Sheringham Park
Refreshments:	Pubs and cafés at Sheringham, pub at Upper Sheringham
Ordnance Survey maps:	Landranger 133 (North East Norfolk) and Pathfinder 820, TG 04/14 (Sheringham & Blakeney)

General description *The beautiful woodland of Sheringham Park is at its best in springtime and early summer when the rhododendrons are in bloom. Many of these are rare varieties specially collected from the Himalayas in the mid-nineteenth century for the owner of Sheringham Hall, Mr Upcher. The woods also have an abundance of bluebells and daffodils. After this wonderful start the route maintains interest through its variety. A fine walk along high (for Norfolk) clifftops follows the section through the park, and leads to Sheringham promenade, with an opportunity to look at the Edwardian resort. A climb to the vantage point of Beeston Hill marks the start of the second part of the route, which returns to the park through woodland and by quiet lanes.*

At the start follow the blue and red waymarked route, entering the woodland to the left of the car park. A field is on the left and the path makes a steep descent into a dell with banks of rhododendrons. The trees

Rhododendrons in Sheringham Park

have suffered some storm damage and there has been considerable replanting. The blue route goes off to the right by a tall oak and a V-shaped beech, but we continue to follow the red arrows and pass some chestnuts of a wonderful size. After a pond the path climbs up to a vantage point with more rhododendrons at the top. The prospect here is being restored to the one sketched by Repton, the designer of the park, in his Red Book.

Join the drive to Sheringham Hall here — dogs should be on leads from this point through the parkland — but turn left before the hall to reach a stile giving onto a field-edge track. This runs by Oak Wood; a path (**A**) on the right into this wood leads up to the Gazebo — the path must be one of the

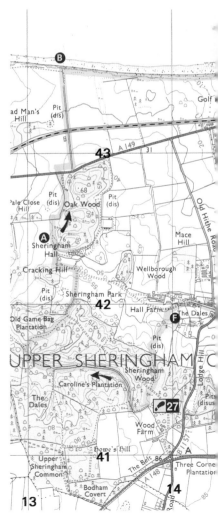

steepest in the county. The Gazebo's original wooden structure was replaced in 1988 by the present steel tower, which is a magnificent viewpoint for coastline and park.

Returning to the track from the Gazebo, turn right to reach the road. Cross this to a path which runs parallel to the road along another field edge and joins with a track going seawards. Note the ruinous pebble-built barn on the left before the railway bridge over the North Norfolk Railway, a preserved section of the old Midland & Great Northern. On the cliff edge turn right onto the Norfolk Coast Path (**B**).

The cliffs are very unstable, so keep well away from the edge. At a height of 165 feet (50 m) or so they are among the highest in Norfolk. National Trust land is left when the path reaches the golf course. Keep to the coast path, which dips and then climbs to a coastguard lookout before it reaches the Sheringham promenade. There is an opportunity to walk on the shore, but since the beach is made up of small, round pebbles progress will be slow.

Remain on the upper promenade until, opposite the Burlington Hotel, steps lead down to the lower promenade. Keep on this, past the centre of the resort, to a toilet block faced with bright yellow tiles. Climb up the steps here to a concrete drive, and bear left off this at a signpost to Beeston Hill, at a putting green (**C**).

The path climbs up to the triangulation point, a viewpoint rivalling the Gazebo earlier in the walk. From here the coast path

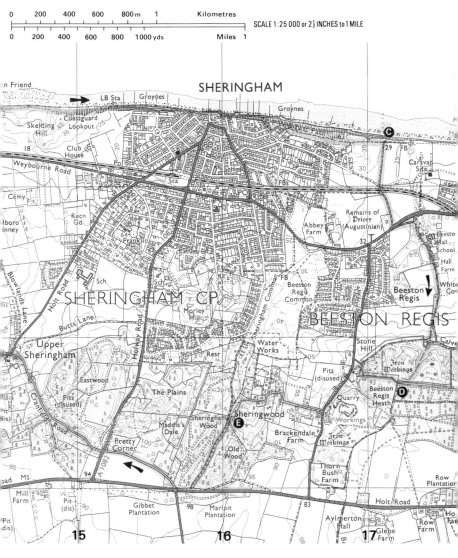

SCALE 1:25 000 or 2½ INCHES to 1 MILE

73

The cliff-top path at Sheringham

descends to a caravan park and a view of the lovely Beeston church. Turn right at the boundary fence to cross the railway and reach the road.

Turn left for about 20 yards (18 m) and then cross to an old section of the main road, which leads to another caravan site. Turn right at the post-box onto a track which leads past Beeston Hall School. Hall Farm has walls made of seashore pebbles, skilfully laid. The track climbs towards woods.

Leave the Norfolk Coast Path when the woods are reached, and take the path straight ahead into them. This is a bridleway well used by horse-riders. Turn right when this path reaches a fence (**D**) and keep this on the left. This is level walking on a heathy ridge with young trees on each side. The path soon descends steeply to reach a lane.

Turn left, and after the Carter Concrete works on the left turn right on the track to Sheringwood. This driveway is twisty. Bear right and then fork left, ignoring signs to Owls Oak, Breckland and Sandywood. Bear left past Robin Hill to pass Bramble Cottage and so reach the track into the woods, with a boundary fence on the left.

Fork right, dropping to a path at the bottom of the dell, and turn left onto this following a yellow, white and blue waymark. When this path meets with another path crossing it (there are red, white and blue arrows on a waymark here (**E**) which should be ignored) go directly over to a very straight embanked track. This climbs, steeply at the end, to the main road. Turn right, and then right again at the crossroads onto the lane leading to Pretty Corner.

This is a famous beauty spot, and easy access to the acres of woodland and heath makes it very popular. Cross another road beyond the car park and walk down Cranfield Road into Upper Sheringham. Pass the post office, pub and church, all on the left, and where the Holt road goes off to the left keep on the Weybourne road for a few yards, before continuing straight on into a cul-de-sac leading to a gate into Sheringham Park.

About 200 yards (183 m) beyond the gate turn to the left (**F**) off the drive, following a red waymark up to the Temple. This was erected by Mr Upcher in 1975. Follow the orange and red waymark on its far side to descend the hill and reach a stile leading out of the park into the woods. A steep climb follows to reach the other drive. Cross this, still following waymarks, now red, blue and orange, to reach the car park.

28 Thorpeness, Friston and the Sailors' Path

Start:	Thorpeness
Distance:	11½ miles (18·5 km)
Approximate time:	4½ hours
Parking:	Car park at the Meare, Thorpeness
Refreshments:	Pub at Friston, tearoom at Thorpeness
Ordnance Survey maps:	Landranger 156 (Saxmundham & Aldeburgh) and Pathfinder 1009, TM 44/45 (Aldeburgh & Orford)

General description *Thorpeness is a remarkable village begun by playwright and barrister Glencairn Stuart Ogilvie shortly before the First World War. He grouped houses, mainly built in a variety of Tudor styles intended to reflect 'Merrie England', around an artificial lake named the Meare and let them to holidaymakers – a sort of East Anglian Portmeirion. Today the houses are privately owned but remain pleasingly eccentric. From this unusual starting point the walk progresses across heath and coppice to the byway village of Friston. It returns on the Sailors' Path, a long stretch of footpath through lovely woodland giving tantalising glimpses of the river and sea.*

Refer to map overleaf.

From the car park at Thorpeness walk round the eastern edge of the Meare and past the road to the golf club. Immediately after this look for a footpath sign on the left; this path follows the edge of the common, behind the houses. The famous House in the Clouds, originally a water-tower, and the post-mill which was moved to the site in 1924 are on the right. Pass to the right of the golf clubhouse, which is also a hotel, and follow the path along the left-hand edge of the golf-course. What appears to be a delightful stretch of river is on the left – it is actually a part of the Meare.

Turn left at Sheepwash Crossing (**A**) onto a narrow path running beside the old railway track. This passes through wild scrubland, with the western part of the artificial lake on the left. Cross a bridge and then turn right off the railway embankment when barbed wire blocks the way ahead. The path now enters a thicket; follow the waymarks – wooden posts with yellow tops. Fork right when the broad path emerges onto open heathland and divides (**B**), and head towards the radio mast which can be seen ahead rising above the trees.

The path skirts the edge of the heath, with a wood of birch and young oaks on the right. This soon gives way to the reedy wilderness called the Fens. Keep straight on when a north to south footpath crosses, and when the path meets the Aldeburgh to Leiston road (the signpost here points to Nuttery Lane), onto a broad, sandy track.

After the drive to Heath House there is heathland on the right and some free-range pigs on the left. The radio mast can now be clearly seen ahead. The farm on the right has peacocks; beyond it the route is on a bridleway across open country towards Portobella Covert, which, perhaps a victim of the storms, has been cleared.

Turn right at Foxburrow Covert (**C**) onto Nuttery Lane, a bridleway leading towards Leiston. This is a lovely track, with fine oaks growing each side, which leads past a pink-washed cottage which bears the name Billeaford Hall. After this the track is metalled and it soon reaches the road at Knodishall Common. Turn left here and at the 30 mph sign, after 200 yards (183 m), take the field-edge path on the right (**D**), following a circular walk waymark. The track becomes

A celebrated landmark – the House in the Clouds at Thorpeness

more pleasing after a footpath from Knodishall joins on the right, with a fine mature hedge on the left. After fields known as Watch Walk Whin the way is across stark, hedgeless fields leading towards Friston church. At the end of the farm track cross the road into Church Lane. Friston church is usually locked; it has an unusual tower with empty niches around the belfry. After the church take the footpath which runs past the village hall and a playing-field to reach the centre of the village at the Old Chequers pub.

Cross the road and take Mill Road, to the right of the pub, passing the sail-less windmill, the tallest post-mill in the county. Where the houses end the road bends to the left, but follow the waymark on the right here (**E**) to cross the large field diagonally. At the far side cross the broad grassy lane, which

was once the drive to Friston Hall, and walk to the left of the hedge. Snape church lies ahead. Turn left at the end of the field onto a short track to the main road.

Go across to a byroad opposite. The wood on the left has been devastated by storms. The quiet lane leads past the barns and sheds of Rookery Farm and turns sharply to the right. At this fiveways (**F**), the route goes to the left on the middle of the three paths, towards a red-brick house, on the signposted Sailors' Path.

The route is now well waymarked as the Suffolk Coast Path. It is disappointing not to be able to see more of the river on the right, but in compensation the path passes through woodland which provides a good habitat for wildlife. The trees are mainly young pines and birches. Interesting landmarks are the bridges

SCALE 1:30 120 or about 2 INCHES to 1 MILE

which cross the marshy land east of Black Heath, and the eerie ruined house in the woods after the last of these bridges and stiles. Subsequently the Sailors' Path follows the driveway from this house, leaving it after another ruined house when, with the main road in sight, it bears to the right along a sunken length of track which proves the antiquity of the path. There is a lovely view of the river from here.

Turn right onto the main road, which has a reasonably wide verge. The road divides Aldeburgh golf-course. Continue past the clubhouse and the first handful of residences. Turn left at a gap in these (**G**) along a private road waymarked with the Suffolk Coast Path sign. After about 400 yards (366 m) look for the imposing white gates of the Red House on the right. This was once the home of

Benjamin Britten and Peter Pears and now contains a library commemorating them. Opposite the gates a footpath strikes across the fairways of the golf-course, heading just to the right of a clump of Scots pines on the other side — the yellow logo of the Suffolk Coast Path is just discernible by an electricity pole. Cross the road onto the track called Warren Hill Lane, which leads past several desirable residences before coming to the old railway line, which it crosses to a marsh track which soon heads towards the shore.

Cross the road at the end of this delightful path and head north back towards Thorpeness, either on the shingle bank or on the sward which lies behind it. A board walk leads through a gap between the shoreline bungalows directly into the car park opposite the Meare.

Useful organisations

The Countryside Commission,
John Dower House, Crescent Place,
Cheltenham, Gloucestershire GL50 3RA.
Tel: 0242 521381

The National Trust,
36 Queen Anne's Gate,
London SW1H 9AS. Tel: 071 222 9251
(East Anglia Regional Office, Blickling,
Norwich NR11 6NF. Tel: 0263 733471)

East Anglia Tourist Board,
Toppesfield Hall, Hadleigh,
Suffolk IP7 7DN. Tel: 0473 822922

Council for National Parks,
246 Lavender Hill, London
SW11 1LJ. Tel: 071 924 4077

The Broads Authority,
18 Colegate, Norwich NR3 1BQ.
Tel: 0603 610734

Broads Authority Information Centres can be found at:
Beccles (Tel: 0502 713196)
Great Yarmouth (Tel: 0493 332095)
Hoveton/Wroxham (Tel: 0603 782281)
Ranworth (Tel: 060 549 453)

Norfolk County Council,
Highways Department, County Hall,
Martineau Lane, Norwich NR1 2DH.
Tel: 0603 223284
(For publications:
Department of Planning and Property,
County Hall, Norwich NR1 2DH.
Tel: 0603 222718)

Suffolk County Council,
Highways Department, St Edmund House,
County Hall, Ipswich IP4 1LZ.
Tel: 0473 230000
(For publications:
Planning Department, St Edmund House,
County Hall, Ipswich IP4 1LZ.
Tel: 0473 265181)

The Forestry Commission,
Information Branch, 231 Corstorphine Road,
Edinburgh EH12 7AT.
Tel: 031 334 0303
(Thetford Forest District Office,
Santon Downham, Brandon,
Suffolk IP27 0TJ. Tel: 0842 810271)

The Ramblers' Association,
1/5 Wandsworth Road, London SW8 2LJ.
Tel: 071 582 6878

The Youth Hostels Association,
Trevelyan House, 8 St Stephen's Hill,
St Albans, Hertfordshire AL1 2DY.
Tel: 0727 855215

The Long Distance Walkers' Association,
7 Ford Drive, Yarnfield, Stone,
Staffordshire ST15 0RP

The Council for the Protection of Rural England,
Warwick House, 25 Buckingham Palace Road,
London SW1W 0PP.
Tel: 071 976 6433

Ordnance Survey,
Romsey Road, Maybush,
Southampton SO9 4DH.
Tel: 0703 792763/4/5 or 792792

Ordnance Survey maps of Norfolk and Suffolk

Norfolk and Suffolk are covered by Ordnance Survey 1:50 000 scale (1¼ inches to 1 mile) Landranger map sheets 132, 133, 134, 144, 155, 156, 168, and 169. These all-purpose maps are packed with information to help you explore the area. Viewpoints, picnic sites, places of interest, caravan and camping sites are shown, as well as public rights of way information such as footpaths and bridle-ways.

To examine Norfolk and Suffolk in more detail and especially if you are planning walks, Ordnance Survey Pathfinder maps at 1:25 000 (2½ inches to 1 mile) scale are ideal. Maps covering this area are:

818 (TF 64/74)
819 (TF 84/94)
820 (TG 04/14)
839 (TF 63/73)
840 (TF 83/93)
841 (TG 03/13)
842 (TG 23/33)

859 (TF 62/72)
860 (TF 82/92)
861 (TG 02/12)
862 (TG 22/32)
863 (TG 42)
880 (TF 61/71)
881 (TF 81/91)

882 (TG 01/11)
883 (TG 21/31)
884 (TG 41/51)
900 (TF 60/70)
901 (TF 80/90)
902 (TG 00/10)
903 (TG 20/30)
904 (TG 40/50)
921 (TL 69/79)
922 (TL 89/99)
923 (TM 09/19)
924 (TM 29/39)
925 (TM 49/59)
942 (TL 68/78)
943 (TL 88/98)
944 (TM 08/18)
945 (TM 28/38)
946 (TM 48/58)
962 (TL 67/77)
963 (TL 87/97)
964 (TM 07/17)

965 (TM 27/37)
966 (TM 47/57)
983 (TL 66/76)
984 (TL 86/96)
985 (TM 06/16)
986 (TM 26/36)
987 (TM 46)
1005 (TL 65/75)
1006 (TL 85/95)
1007 (TM 05/15)
1008 (TM 25/35)
1009 (TM 44/45)
1028 (TL 64/74)
1029 (TL 84/94)
1030 (TM 04/14)
1031 (TM 24/34)
1051 (TL 63/73)
1052 (TL 83/93)
1053 (TM 03/13)
1054 (TM 23/33)

To get to Norfolk and Suffolk, use the Ordnance Survey Routemaster map number 9 South East England at 1:250 000 (1 inch to 4 miles) scale.

Ordnance Survey maps and guides are available from most booksellers, stationers and newsagents.